The CINCINNATI Neighborhood Guidebook

The CINCINNATI Neighborhood Guidebook

Edited by Nick Swartsell

Copyright © 2022, Belt Publishing
All rights reserved. This book or any portion thereof may not be reproduced or used in any manner whatsoever without the express written permission of the publisher except for the use of brief quotations in a book review.

First Edition 2022
ISBN: 9781953368447

Belt Publishing
5322 Fleet Avenue, Cleveland, OH 44105
www.beltpublishing.com

Book design by Meredith Pangrace
Cover by David Wilson

CONTENTS

Introduction
Nick Swartsell 11

CENTRAL

Over-the-Rhine: The Crossroads at Fourteenth and Vine
Michael Henson 15

The West End: 2020 Vision
Cailin Pitt 18

Queensgate: Cincinnati's Front Door at Union Terminal
Pauletta Hansel 21

Downtown: Downtown versus the Central Business District
Nick Swartsell 25

Court Street District: On its Own Downtown
Bonnie Speeg Holliday 30

Brighton: Memories of the Baymiller Pedestrian Bridge
Jon Carter 33

Mount Adams: Life on the Hill
Liz Gottmer 35

UPTOWN

Avondale: It Takes a Village
Deqah Hussein-Wetzel 41

North Avondale: Satisfaction in the Effort
Julie Zimmerman 44

Clifton: "That's Not Clifton"
Anne Skove 47

Burnet Woods: Ducks on a Pond
Anne Delano Steinert 50

Mount Auburn: On Rice Street
Nick Swartsell 53

WEST

The Mill Creek Valley: Illuminating Obstacles
Elissa Yancey 61

Camp Washington: An Island in the Stream
Jocelyn Gibson 64

East Westwood: Where the Sidewalk Ends
Annette J. Wick 67

The Price Hills: Diaspora from the Bottoms
Sarah Thomas 70

Westwood: More than Cincinnati's Texas
Greg Hand 73

EAST

Evanston: Hope after the Highway
Carrie Rhodus 79

Hyde Park East: Funky for a Hundred Years
Dann Woellert 82

Mount Lookout: The Lights of My Neighbors
Rob Pasquinucci 86

CONTENTS

Madisonville: The Double Bind
Eric Eble 88

East Walnut Hills: The Parade
Kathy Y. Wilson 93

Mount Washington: Front Yard City, Backyard Suburb
Michael Henson 97

Camp Dennison: A Hidden Gem Fading
Dani McClain 99

SOUTH

Covington: The End of an Era at City Heights
Briana Rice 105

Ludlow: Grounded by the River
Katrina Eresman 108

Bellevue: Heaven in Bellevue
Caitlyn Short 112

Newport: The Lost Story of a Workers' Strike
Thurman Wenzl 116

NORTH

Carthage: Four Cultures, Four Congregations
Rev. Alan Dicken 123

Northside: Honeysuckle and Urban Streams
Katie Vogel 126

College Hill: Big in Abolition, Big in Japan
Gail Finke 129

**Forest Park/Fairfield: The Death and Life
of American Malls**
Ronny Salerno 132

St. Bernard: Twenty-Four-Karat Service
Nicole R. Klungle 137

**Greenhills: Kneeling for Black Lives in a Town
Born Segregated**
Nick Swartsell 141

Norwood: A Kingdom Unto Itself
Angela Pancella 144

Lockland: Rust Belt Dream Come True
Alexander C. Smith 146

Contributors 151

Introduction

NICK SWARTSELL

Hello, dear reader, and thank you for picking up *The Cincinnati Neighborhood Guidebook*. Glad to have you along on this textual tour of the Queen City.

First, let's talk about what this book is not. You won't find profiles of the hottest neighborhoods in which to buy a home or lists of their newest bars, restaurants, and cultural amenities. Other publications do that ably and more nimbly than this tome could. By the time we get it into publication, much of that information will have changed anyway.

This slim volume is also not at all an exhaustive study of all the city's fifty-two neighborhoods, countless subneighborhoods, outlying suburbs, and other geographic points of interest. Each community has its own stories, its own fascinating character (and characters), and each one deserves to be celebrated, to be sure. But that would be a large volume, and you, dear reader, as attentive and curious as you are, would likely skip to something familiar or attention grabbing eventually.

Instead, this book is just a sampling written by those who answered the call for submissions and felt passionately that you simply must know *something* about the way life feels—and why it feels that way—in their communities. You will likely be able to think of communities this book should have included, and you would be right. In thinking so, you will have developed an idea for a submission the editor of some future sequel will gratefully welcome.

That leads me to the heart of the matter: this book is wonderfully and purposefully neither cohesive nor conclusive. It's a short, open-ended series of missives from very different places that are changing, and because they are changing, they are hard to freeze in time or fit together into an easy pattern. In short, they are places that are alive.

Thus, the happy job of this book is not to sum up but to complicate your understanding of Cincinnati.

I can think of nothing more fitting for this city, which sits on land once occupied by multiple groups of Indigenous people and which started out its current iteration as not one but three lonely and different settlements along the Ohio River. Even the first name for the town these settlements eventually became—Losantiville—describes its location across from the Licking River using Greek, Latin, French, and English. A real grab bag we are here.

The name "Cincinnati" was an attempt by very early leaders to give this place a more unified and noble identity. But even the story of Cincinnatus—the Roman farmer who left his fields to command an army, only to refuse the reins of power when the war was over—speaks of duality and adaptability, of fluid identity.

And that's what Cincinnati is all about. Long seen as a place a decade behind the times, we've grappled with serious urban issues ahead of the rest of the nation. Corrupt leaders at the turn of the twentieth century sparked reform efforts that led to one of the first instances of council-manager municipal governance. City leaders drew up one of the United States' first comprehensive municipal plans here in 1925.

Sometimes being ahead of the major issues is tragic. A decade and a half before the Black Lives Matter movement, a Cincinnati police officer shot an unarmed Black man, pushing a group of dedicated activists to win some of the nation's first and most recognized modern police reforms. Those same activists are still fighting to have those reforms honored.

As I write this, a new mayor and an almost entirely new Cincinnati City Council are just warming up after a tumultuous few years for city government that featured another round of corruption scandals, battles over a number of serious issues, and not a little over-the-top political theater. Will our new elected leaders take higher roads? We shall see. Even if they do, those roads are likely to diverge.

We are a city of stories and counter-stories, where small towns atop hills and those nestled in valleys are welded together and kept separate by accident and annexation, by ancient geologic forces and grudges that feel nearly as old. Here you may think of the city's cliché clashes—East Side versus West Side, Skyline versus Goldstar chili, pro- versus anti-streetcar.

But I would like to submit that these near-tectonic frictions are what keeps Cincinnati churning, evolving, and energized.

In short, all of this difference is what makes this city so alive. Here is a sampling of that life—the tensions, the changes, the debates, the life-and-death battles, and, not least of all, the joys we share.

CENTRAL

Over-the-Rhine: The Crossroads at Fourteenth and Vine

MICHAEL HENSON

On a bright, bitter cold day some thirty years ago, long before Over-the-Rhine had been gentrified into OTR, I watched a woman and four children gather to cross at Fourteenth and Vine. Around them were the traffic in motion on Vine, the traffic at rest on Fourteenth, the vigilant and reposed drug dealers leaning against the boarded windows of the pool hall, the walkers with their canes or their strollers or their bags of groceries. Around them all was a maze of brick and neon, signboards, walk lights, glass, vinyl, plywood, chrome, paper, asphalt, plastic, and, in the path of a passing truck, a plume of diesel smoke descending.

The corner of Fourteenth and Vine in Cincinnati was then, and still is, a busy corner. The bar on the southeast corner is still a bar, but it now serves sushi and sake. The abandoned pool hall across Vine is now a gourmet donut shop. All manner of people have come and gone across this particular intersection. But I have carried in my mind the image of this woman and these children almost photographically for all these many years.

They have stayed with me, in part, I suppose, because of a little riff of drama between the woman, who seemed tipsy, and the oldest of the children, a preadolescent girl with a proud, wary eye.

The woman was white, the children were Black, and it seemed the woman was an interloper in this scene. She looked like someone's grandmother, but she did not look like theirs. And the oldest girl, who may have been twelve, was clearly in charge of these children. She had linked them, hand to hand, and lined them up at the curb like marchers in a parade. They were packed identically in bright insulated coats, hooded, bundled, and immobilized like fine china packed for shipping. They were bright-colored beauties, admirably protected and prepared for the bitter cold air of Vine Street.

But the woman was bare-handed, dressed shabbily, out of season and out of fashion in a camel-colored cloth coat with a kerchief knotted at her chin.

Twenty years earlier, she would not have looked out of place, for she would have looked like many women among the thousands of white and Black Appalachian migrants who then shared this neighborhood with growing numbers of African Americans displaced from the West End. The woman reminded me of women I have seen in coal camps, in country stores, or outside storefront churches on Wednesday nights after services—knotty, strong-minded, sharp-tongued women, hard-scrabble matriarchs, the moral and emotional centers of struggling, displaced families. They are women of great density, made solid by grief and wisdom.

But this woman had lost that solidity. She was the center, it seemed, of nothing. She teetered unsteadily to the right, then back to the left, then again to the right as she leaned toward the youngest child, the wide-eyed one, and extended a shaky hand to take him by the mitten. For a moment, as the old woman wobbled, it seemed she might mislead this wide-eyed one into the teeth of the traffic.

The girl, from her end of the line, watched with her wary eye.

Terrible things have happened at the corner of Fourteenth and Vine. Some of them have been the major, get-in-the-news terrible—traffic accidents, robberies, shootings, and the like. Just a few blocks away, police bullets killed a nineteen-year-old Black man named Timothy Thomas in 2001, setting off four days of insurrection. A few blocks beyond that was the homeless shelter where my friend, the housing activist buddy gray was shot and killed by a client he had befriended. Two blocks in the other direction is the spot where musician Michael Bany was killed after a Main Street gig. But most are the small, usual, almost manageable, easily unnoticed sort of terrible in which, day after day, amidst such physical and moral damage and such daily disillusionment, addicts drift hollowly toward the next fix, young men waste arrogantly on the corners, and young women become young mothers become prostitutes.

But the terrible stories have never been the whole story of Over-the-Rhine. There have always been many, mostly untold stories of survival, resilience, and even triumph in these streets. Schools, churches, social service centers, and individual families offer protective havens. Dotted here and there in the neighborhood are a number of halfway houses, treatment centers, and transitional housing units where the work of recovery hums along. There are innocence and strength in these streets, but they tend to remain quietly in the background. Little of this is out front; none of it is as vivid and compelling as what is out on the corner, where damaged and corrupted life staggers, weaves, toddles, struts, pimp walks, and cruises by at every hour.

I first moved into Over-the-Rhine in the summer of 1968. I lived there, volunteered there, or worked there for many of the years after. I got to know many of its odd corners and its interesting (and sometimes odd) people. Over the years, the original German, Irish, and Italian immigrants who once lived there were replaced by Appalachian and African American migrants who are now being replaced by a culturally diverse group of workers, artists, entrepreneurs, and investors whose experiences, interests, income levels, and access to resources and power are, in the main, vastly different from those of the people I met there over fifty years ago.

If we consider the neighborhood to be a particular collection of buildings, streets, and other physical structures, then Over-the-Rhine is cleaner, safer, and richer than it has ever been. The new people bring their new hopes and energies to the neighborhood. But I wonder if they know anything of the hopes, energies, and struggles of people of the other Over-the-Rhine, of those like the little group I saw at Fourteenth and Vine that day. I would like to think they care.

I would like to think, as Over-the-Rhine continues to see new intersections and transformations, that its new people will reach out, like that old woman long ago, to help others cross.

The West End: 2020 Vision
CAILIN PITT

Sixty years ago, a major section of the West End (a Cincinnati, Ohio, neighborhood) was bulldozed and flattened so a new neighborhood and interstate highway could be built through it. The new neighborhood would be called Queensgate, and the new highway would be called I-75. This urban renewal project would be called Kenyon-Barr (named after two streets in the neighborhoods located in the scope of the project), and it would lead to the displacement of more than 25,000 residents, 97 percent of whom were nonwhite.

The Kenyon-Barr project sort of had good intentions. In a post-World War II society, many people were leaving cities and moving to new subdivisions in the suburbs, which led to a loss of tax revenue for cities. If cities weren't able to stem the loss of revenue, it could lead to a lot of bad things, like not being able to afford essential services.

The federal government was deep in the effort of building a nationwide network of highways, and it was planning to build several throughout the Cincinnati region, including the Mill Creek Expressway (I-75). To attract industrial companies to move inside the city limits, the city of Cincinnati had the idea of creating a new neighborhood located right by one of the new highways, which would allow companies located there to easily transport goods and services. By creating Queensgate, and by having new industrial companies, there would be an increase of jobs within the city limits and increased tax revenue. Having I-75 run through the city would in theory allow people to drive to their destinations faster and decrease congestion on city roads.

Unfortunately, these plans hinged on the destruction of the heart of Cincinnati's Black community. The West End at the time was a dense, thriving, and vibrant community that was slowly destroyed so Queensgate and I-75 could be built. The people who lived in the West End did not have the ability to fight back against the urban renewal project like other whiter and wealthier neighborhoods in the city might have been able to. Impacted West End residents were also promised better housing and amenities if they supported the project. Over six years, the Kenyon-Barr project demolished most of the West End to create Queensgate and make way for I-75. As of 2010, only 6,627 people live in the West End, and 142 people live in

Queensgate, as most of Queensgate is now home to industrial businesses and warehouses. The city photographed many of the buildings located in the West End before they were destroyed by the project.

I moved to the West End in October 2018, after living in Mariemont (an affluent Cincinnati suburb) and Hyde Park (another affluent Cincinnati neighborhood). I love the West End because it's beautiful and unique. My apartment building was built in the late nineteenth century, and judging from historical photos I've been able to find, my apartment unit used to be a barbershop. Streetcar tracks used to be on my street, and there used to be a Car Barn down the road, where streetcars were housed and serviced.

The West End is one of the poorest neighborhoods in Cincinnati, but it has a better sense of community and nicer people than the more "well-off" places I've lived in Cincinnati. I learned about the Kenyon-Barr project before I moved to the West End, and it broke my heart to learn about something that caused so much heartache and pain for the people who lived in this neighborhood before me, just so I could have the luxury to sit in I-75 traffic every day.

One of the hardest things about living in the West End was knowing what used to be here before urban renewal and years of disinvestment from the city. Whenever I look at old pictures of the West End from the forties and fifties, I see a thriving, beautiful, and dense neighborhood. One of the reasons the West End was destroyed was because even though it was a thriving neighborhood, the people who lived here at the time were deemed not important enough. American urban renewal projects during this time were rooted in racism and classism. Most Interstate highways that snake through cities were routed through neighborhoods that used to house nonwhite people because it was cheaper to acquire their homes and neighborhoods than white and wealthier ones.

Another hard part for me about living in the West End was knowing what the people who were displaced from here faced when they had to leave. Redlining was still legal during the time the Kenyon-Barr project occurred, which meant Black Cincinnatians had an extremely limited supply of neighborhoods in the city they were able to find homes in. To address displacement caused by the project, the city planned to build new public housing to house the former West End residents. Unfortunately, the public housing that was eventually built was nowhere near enough to house everyone who was displaced, and some of the limited housing built was segregated, meaning almost all of the people displaced from the West End were excluded from living there.

Some people were able to move into already integrated neighborhoods like Avondale and Mount Auburn, but many families had to leave the city of Cincinnati entirely because they couldn't find new homes in the city. I can't imagine how hard it must have been to lose your home and have to leave all of your friends and everything familiar to you simply because of your skin color.

Another hard part about living in the West End was knowing that sixty years later, the Kenyon-Barr project was a complete failure. Queensgate is an extremely undesirable place to be. Apart from Union Terminal, the rest of the neighborhood is full of unfriendly warehouses, wide roads, and giant, nondescript buildings.

To be fair, this was probably exactly what the city wanted Queensgate to become when the Kenyon-Barr project was born, but I still consider it to be a failure to have a giant neighborhood in the urban core no one wants to be in. I also consider I-75 to be a failure. The people who envisioned the American interstate system wanted it to be an efficient system to get people from Point A to Point B and relieve congestion from city streets. Sixty years later, we've seen that highways have encouraged more and more people to drive, increasing congestion. In my opinion, all of the positives Queensgate and I-75 may have brought to Cincinnati will never be enough to justify the human cost of displacing over 25,000 people.

Unfortunately, this piece doesn't have a happy ending. I could see I-75 from my bedroom window, and it served as a constant reminder to me of the Kenyon-Barr project. I can't help but imagine what the West End could have been had the project never happened. In 2020, apart from the main thoroughfares like Linn Street and Liberty Avenue, most of the neighborhood is usually dead. After decades of disinvestment and lack of attention from the city and general public, the West End started to receive awareness again when FC Cincinnati announced they wanted to build a new soccer stadium here.

Money was finally going to start pouring into the neighborhood again, and surely people would have a reason to visit! Unfortunately, that attention has come with a lot of worry, as many West End residents are concerned the new stadium and the plans FC Cincinnati have for the area will result in gentrification and displacement—in fact, some residents have already been displaced due to living near the stadium footprint.

My hope is that more people will learn about the places where they live and apply those lessons to the future.

This essay first appeared on the author's website, cailinpitt.com.

Queensgate: Cincinnati's Front Door at Union Terminal

PAULETTA HANSEL

The first time I saw Union Terminal, Cincinnati's art deco train station, was in 1977 on a midnight side trip during my first visit to Cincinnati. I was on my way to the Amtrak Station on River Road to catch the train home to West Virginia. Before that trip, both cities and trains were only distant promises, a long low whistle in the night. The terminal back then was empty, dark, and beautiful. I thought it looked like one of those mantle clocks from the twenties or thirties, wood turned dusky with age, all rounded edges on a solid base. I gave no thought to the neighborhood in which it was located. The Appalachian towns where I'd grown up were too small to have neighborhoods with names.

Queensgate is the name the city gave that area back in the 1960s, after they had torn most of it down. First, they renamed that section of the West End community "Kenyon-Barr" after two of the streets to be razed, making way for I-75 and the bleak industrial park that now surrounds it. Union Terminal predates it all.

Before Union Terminal, there were five passenger stations around the city. Planning for a consolidated station began around the turn of the twentieth century. Had Union Terminal been built when it was needed, it would have been some neoclassical structure. Instead, ground was broken in 1929, the heart of art deco design, just before the stock market crashed, and as automobiles and even airplanes were beginning to take the place of trains.

After my move to Cincinnati in 1979, a half century after Union Terminal's initial construction began, I continued to see it as a place separate from the era and the location in which it sat. I loved the place at a whimsical distance.

My friend Paul Morris, before he lost his job during the COVID-19 pandemic, loved it close up, from the inside out. Paul started his work at the terminal as an actor in a living history exhibit in the museum center's special exhibition hall, and he stayed on to work security in the living history that is Union Terminal itself.

Although Amtrak brought its station back not long after the Cincinnati Museum Center moved there in 1990, I have never taken a train from the terminal nor had the opportunity to spend much time beneath its domed roof: a few visits to the erstwhile shopping mall; an interminable avant-garde 1980s film festival in the News Reel Theatre; a fancy-dress dinner dance a few decades later; an occasional visit to the Omnimax; or to just walk and gawk.

So in June 2016, a few weeks before Union Terminal closed for a two-year major renovation project, when Paul offered to take me on a grand behind-the-scenes tour, I was thrilled.

On our tour, Paul took me up into the rotunda, where I could only think of the past. My mother, as a girl of twelve, stood twice where I now stood, passing through in 1944 from the creek beds of Kentucky on her way to Buffalo—the Niagara River's and Lake Erie's shores—and back again in 1945.

The week before my tour with Paul, my husband and I had wheeled her around the place. She told me once that what struck her most during her trip were all the pretty dresses, cut on a bias and with hems up almost to the knees, saving fabric for the war effort. Before she died, she had dementia—whatever she remembered about this or anywhere she has traveled was locked inside her brain. I sent her with my husband to the "Whispering Fountain" at one side of the rotunda's arch and from the other, called to her, "Hello, hello!" My voice carried up along the grooves of the arch and back down to her. I was calling to the past. She didn't answer.

Behind the rotunda's dome, everything, Paul told me, is all "crosses and leans"—not a vertical line to be seen. I tell him he is a poet, as well as an actor and security guard. I can't take it all in. It takes me in. Paul snapped a picture of me looking out the window over the rotunda, above the terminal's famed murals of men marching from the past to some vison of who we would be, a dream of the future that now exists only on these walls.

Paul showed me the hooks from which the flag drapes. Back in the fifties, some automobile dealership hung a car on a platform from the hooks, showing off their wares. Down below, beneath the floor of the rotunda, is where cars and buses deposited their passengers who would walk up the long ramp and on back to the concourses and out to the platforms to wait for the trains. Now the concourse is gone and only one platform still exists.

This place invited in the cancer that would kill its purpose for being. On the murals, there are no images of cars.

Back down a set of stairs and a creaking elevator, time has seeped into the cork walls of the Railroad Association board room; it smells like the inside of a cigar box. I closed my eyes to see the men around the ornate table, their bald heads vulnerable without fedoras, making their soon-to-be antiquated plans. Did they know—even as they looked around them, saw that it was good—that their time had nearly come?

In the president's office, Paul had me walk toward the center where the office chair would have been, counting aloud. My voice grows large and multiplies; I am the great, the powerful. (It is not lost on me that the shopping mall housed briefly in this place had been called the Land of Oz.)

There is a semicircle just inside the door from the association secretary's office; this is as far into the president's sanctum as she was allowed to go. Did she call each new president, "sir"? For thirty years, she kept the keys to 600 doors in a box hung on the wall across from her desk. There is no record of her name.

Paul took me down to see the generators. The boilers and the pipes that run from them were painted hot pink. Nobody knows why, he said. He took me to the room they call the morgue, where they stored the bodies of soldiers coming back from World War II. He told me that the words "check body bags for live ammo" are still painted on the walls. It was too dark for me to see.

Out the terminal's glass front doors, beyond its iconic fountains, it is still hard for me to think of Queensgate as a neighborhood, much less to imagine the bustling African American community that existed there before the city urban-renewed it. Many came here from the south in the decades prior, stepping through Union Terminal on the way to their new homes in the West End. In the 1940s, when my young not-yet mother was traversing the country by rail, the young William Mallory Sr., who went on to become Ohio's first African American majority floor leader, walked from his West End home to collect coins from those fountains and to earn a few cents to watch over the Reds fans' parked cars as they watched the games at the nearby Crosley Field.

In what is left of the West End, the City Gospel Mission, also formerly in the now repurposed Over-the-Rhine, sits beside what was Crosley Field's home plate,

Paradoxically, Union Terminal remains a survivor. And I love it despite—maybe because—obsolescence was written into its DNA. I love how it survives on beauty. It was a museum from its beginnings, built for a function, which, even as men planned its glory, was traveling shiny new tracks backward, toward the rusty past. The last of its kind. The best of its kind. They got everything wrong, these planners for the future, and thus this place, this whispering arch, remains—forever I hope—exactly right.

Downtown: Downtown versus the Central Business District

NICK SWARTSELL

If you want to be official about it, Cincinnati's Central Business District, or CBD—the economic and cultural heart of the city, at least in theory—has very specific boundaries. Central Parkway, the former canal, marks its northern end. Eggleston Avenue, gray and utilitarian, marks most of its eastern boundary, and a jog of city streets its western one. The Ohio River bounds it to the south.

Within those lines, you'll find a lot of things. The city's Contemporary Art Center, designed by world-renowned architect Zaha Hadid, and the Taft Museum, another arts institution housed in the former mansion of one of Cincinnati's first prominent families, are both here. The headquarters of major corporations like Kroger, Procter & Gamble, and Great American Insurance hold court in their various corners of the neighborhood, and myriad other office buildings hum during the weekdays and go dark on evenings and weekends. Fountain Square, sometimes called the city's living room, is here, its locally iconic fountain serving as the city's official symbol.

But the lines that comprise the CBD don't conform neatly to more geologic boundaries, the Mill Creek to the west and the steep, cliff-like hills to the north and east that look down on not just the CBD but also the surrounding dense, older neighborhoods called Over-the-Rhine and the West End.

If you talk to a resident of a certain age who came up in one of these neighborhoods—that is, someone who lives somewhere in that geologic bowl—they will tell you they lived or still live "downtown." It's a different downtown than the Central Business District delineated on the city's neighborhood statistical approximations.

This downtown is home to Stanley Rowe Towers, the fourteen-story Cincinnati Metropolitan Housing Authority development built in 1963. The red and orange concrete towers house more than 300 families and are visible from miles around, one of the few structures of such height outside the Central Business District proper.

When it was built, Stanley Rowe must have seemed like the beginning of a promise kept—new housing for those displaced by urban renewal farther south in the West End. But not much more housing came after it for the rest of the mostly Black residents who were displaced by all that demolition. In the decades since, maintenance has become an increasing challenge there due to the development's advancing age and budget cuts to HUD.

At night, the wind whips around the grounds, carrying steam from the buildings' boilers. Some residents believe the towers' days are numbered—part of a move away from these kinds of developments by HUD.

The housing authority received a grant to plan for the future of the complex in 2020 but hasn't announced the fate of the buildings, saying only that residents will be able to stay in the West End if the towers come down.

Broader "downtown" is also home to Ollie's Trolley, the long-running hamburger stand on Liberty Street. Ollie's sits across the street from the city's new Major League Soccer stadium, which is on land once occupied by a neighborhood soul food restaurant, a historic theater building, a barber shop, and a handful of apartments. All of that was in the West End. But when you asked the residents of those now-gone apartment buildings where they lived, they would tell you downtown.

This downtown is also home to Findlay Market, Ohio's oldest continually operating public food marketplace. It's home to murals by William Rankins Jr., a prolific artist, who in the 1990s and 2000s painted murals featuring pop culture icons like Robocop and Steve Urkel for restaurants, corner stores, and other businesses, many of them Black owned. If you're of a certain generation of Cincinnatian, those murals defined the aesthetics of the downtown zone. Slowly, they are disappearing.

Officially delineated from the Central Business District but playing out in the heart of "downtown" is a nationally recognized redevelopment effort in Over-the-Rhine, a mixture of hundreds of millions of dollars spent on renovations and an extended branding effort promoting the neighborhood's historic architecture, brewing heritage, and "old-world" feel. Less recognized: the fact that this effort coincided with the loss of some 70 percent of the neighborhood's housing that was affordable to low-income residents, and a reduction in its once sizeable Black population.

That change hasn't skipped over the CBD proper, either.

Once, single-room occupancy hotels dotted the CBD, offering bare-bones accommodations for those seeking the most affordable of housing.

The Metropole on Walnut Street in the CBD was the last of those buildings when it was converted to a boutique hotel in 2009. Another boutique hotel occupies the former Anna Louise Inn, which stood for more than 100 years near the aforementioned Taft Mansion as a shelter for women escaping domestic violence and trafficking.

With the changes come questions, and with the questions comes the battle over meaning. What does "downtown" mean, and who decides that?

In short, whether you think of downtown as the Central Business District or as the wider geologic basin says something about your frame of reference for this city and its history. Is your sense of space oriented around where you can easily walk, where you might have relatives or friends, the closest store, the last apartment you lived in? Does downtown for you begin with a highway exit? Is it about a network of people and familiar places or a litany of exciting new developments and centers of social, cultural, or monetary capital?

It is entirely possible, by the way, to hold both views at once or in quick succession. But make no mistake: they are very different frames of reference for determining what "downtown" means.

Few places play host to the meaning-making competitions that define urban life like downtowns do, and the contemporary semantic schism between the Central Business District and "downtown" is just one example in Cincinnati. This bowl carved out by the movement of ancient water and ice has been holding different, competing meanings since humans first set eyes on it.

The Shawnee considered the basin and the Mill Creek Valley bordering it to be the center of the universe. Hundreds of years before that, Indigenous people—likely the Hopewell—built earthworks on land that is now the West End and Over-the-Rhine centerpiece, Washington Park.

White settlers and city makers unceremoniously removed them all in the nineteenth century, focusing on making their own meanings of the land, often violently.

But even the history of those European settlers is a battle of meanings. A few of the Germans who settled in the basin and gave Over-the-Rhine its name became beer barons, yes, but thousands of them were socialist radicals fleeing the failed series of revolutions that swept Europe in the late 1840s. They brought their tendency for political activism with them, starting abolitionist churches and newspapers, and sometimes protesting—even rioting on occasion.

Today, in its rebranded "OTR" form, the brewing heritage is remembered, marketed, and celebrated. The rowdy Forty-Eighters and their radical politics are all but forgotten.

It is not surprising that this battle of meanings often centers around race and politics. Few Cincinnatians know much about the riots of 1836 and 1841, when white mobs chased Black residents out of a section of downtown where they lived into less desirable and flood-prone locations in the West End. The mobs burned houses, killed Black residents, and generally menaced an early Cincinnati Black neighborhood out of existence.

The southern West End those Black residents were forced into became the predominant center for Black life in Cincinnati before urban renewal wiped it off the map.

These erasures—like those of Native peoples—are today mostly forgotten. Instead, the boom of an urban renaissance defines the perception of the Central Business District and downtown more generally.

The narrative, like many others, has its roots in solid truth. New apartments, restaurants, and office buildings pop up at a regular pace downtown. The aforementioned redevelopment of Over-the-Rhine continues, despite a global pandemic that has put a drag on its polished restaurants and boutiques but has only accelerated the sale of its refurbished condos. And after decades of losing, the 2021 AFC Champion Cincinnati Bengals hold court in Paul Brown Stadium in the Central Business District's southwest corner.

But the truth behind the resurgence is also more complicated than the simple meaning city boosters often ascribe to it, and the current dynamism is likely more fragile and ephemeral than they care to admit.

For decades, one of the first things new arrivals would see upon exiting the Union Terminal train station in Queensgate—the very edge of "downtown"—were the proud art deco angles of Carew Tower soaring above the heart of the Central Business District.

Like a lot of magnificent things in Cincinnati, the timing of Carew was, shall we say, less than auspicious, with the construction of the opulent forty-nine-story office building and hotel beginning just a month before the 1929 stock market crash that ushered in the Great Depression.

Carew was something entirely its own. It held the Mabley and Carew department store, the Hilton Netherland Plaza Hotel, a high-class restaurant and bar, live music, and even an indoor ice-skating rink. It presaged indoor malls and let those who could make use of its technologically groundbreaking parking garage partake in the city inside without having to trek through the city outside. It was, so to speak, the central business district of the Central Business District.

It was a stunning and ambitious effort, predating New York City's Rockefeller Center by two years but built on the same concept. It was a symbol of a city that took itself seriously and that wasn't ready to let its former prominence—just a long lifetime prior, Cincinnati was the sixth-largest city in the country—slip away.

And if you squint your eyes while you stand in the Hilton's marble-walled lobby now, you can pretend it didn't slip away at all. The Hilton is still there, its Hall of Mirrors banquet room still lit in its eerie gold glass opulence, its guests still well-heeled and cosmopolitan. Fine murals still line the walls (and ceiling) of the five-star Orchids at the Palm Court restaurant. Locally famous Rookwood tiles in flowery motifs still run floor to ceiling in the building's central arcade.

But there are few shops around that arcade now—just a pretzel stand, a store selling Cincinnati memorabilia, a clothing store or two, and a themed diner where the cultural clock stopped sometime in the early 1960s. Eerie wind whistles through the elevator shafts and stairwells, singing a lonely song in the wild art deco ballrooms.

As of late 2021, the tower's owners faced foreclosure and owed $642,000 in back utility bills. Office tenants have slowly drained from Carew. It is at once opulent and ominous, energetic and empty.

The same could be said for the CBD as a whole. For every new development triumph—downtown's first grocery store in decades, another thirty residential units here, another fifty there—there is a Carew Tower or the similarly historic and much more empty Terrace Plaza Hotel, which is entirely boarded up. And that's not to mention the camps of people without housing under the overpasses that separate the CBD from the stadiums and the Banks.

The wind whistles through Carew, and it whistles through Stanley Rowe, that bastion of West End/downtown Cincinnati living. They are both in flux, both subject to the shifting meanings we ascribe to them and the whims those meanings whip up in us.

Court Street District: On its Own Downtown

BONNIE SPEEG HOLLIDAY

Court Street holds a reputation for its commerce and legal folderol. It is an urban core kind of place, nestled as it is just north of the hustle and bustle of the Central Business District's towers and just south of Over-the-Rhine. So much so that it is a semiregular location for film crews looking to replicate urban environs like 1970s New York City.

Here's the thing: Behind the film sets and the attorneys strolling to the Hamilton County Courthouse, Court Street is a neighborhood. But it's unlike a sleepy enclave in the suburbs.

I lived on Court Street between Main and Elm Street. In part, it shaped who I am. When I'm there, I'm still home. Painters, potters, a former mayor, and a world-famous inventor have all called Court Street home.

The diversity drew me to this corner of downtown. Residences were above businesses, and when I lived there, it was a culturally integrated neighborhood. For a long time, it was one of the few receptive parts of town for gay men, burlesque entertainers, and the enigmatic Vine Street Betty. We lived above the oldest manufacturer of candy canes in the country, Doscher's French Chew Candy Factory. They've since moved to the outskirts in Newtown; their Court Street building is now a pastry shop. When I walk in, I still think I smell peppermint.

On weekends, Court Street is relatively quiet. The county offices are closed, as are most of the businesses. This used to give residents like us a chance to meet for parties with friends who lived in and across the street from the massive Rose Exterminator Building at Walnut and Court (now an enormous downtown grocery store and luxury apartment development).

One building was on the southeast corner, where Charley Harper's bird mural colors its west side. Walking down Court Street now, I feel a bit of a jolt knowing that in 1856, on that same corner, eighteen-year-old genius Thomas Edison roomed at the Bevis House, working as a telegraph operator.

We were not geniuses, but we lived just a few buildings from Edison's old haunt at 24 West Court Street, and we had a serious advantage over our friends who lived in Walnut Hills, Mount Adams, or Clifton Heights.

We would hand the landlady, Elsie Doscher, our $36 rent check in the business office, where years later, John Travolta changed from his boxers into a gangster suit while shooting the *Gotti* movie.

When we moved there fifty years ago, we didn't often have to leave the neighborhood because basic necessities were nearby. We walked to rock concerts at Music Hall; movie theaters were plentiful. Court Street Market, until a decade ago, had Findlay Market vendors set up and down the street on Tuesdays and Thursdays.

Surviving nearby are Avril Bleh's Meats, Cappel's (art supplies, tape, cricket clickers, candles, pirate hats, Mardi Gras feathers), Minges Candy (the Willy Wonka of the street), Bob Sumerall Car Repair, Scotti's Italian Restaurant (like being in Naples but cheaper), and Stavales Tailor, still the charmer of Court Street.

Court Street has the feeling of being on its own. Central Parkway is the separator for the jumbo neighborhood Over-the-Rhine, the wide thoroughfare once a canal with barge boats carrying goods and produce. The wider width of Court Street between Main and Vine is due to the huge public market house once standing there that was built in 1829. That street width remains distinct.

When I walk along Court Street near the new Kroger store, I imagine the small wooden barrels I would see outside storefronts of the Greek grocer at Court and Vine and of the Zoutis Candy down near Walnut. The barrels and the stores are gone, but there's still food nearby.

Brooklyn has a Court Street that looks remarkably similar to Cincinnati's. That could explain why scenes for at least three major films have been shot on Court Street.

"The street retains that old city look," location scouts tell me. Recently, watching the final day of shooting for the soon to be released Shirley Chisholm film *Shirley*, I was asked to take a photo of two film set designers. The filmmaker was using the old Fox's Clothing storefront across the street from my old abode as Chisholm's New York campaign headquarters. We used to buy seventy-five cent T-shirts there in blue or green when the laundromat broke.

Fox's was also featured in Todd Haynes's movie *Carol*. Their cool sign is now at the American Sign Museum out in Camp Washington. I told the set designers, "I used to live right over there when Chisholm ran for president in the 1970s." They said, "Well, whoa, take a shot of us in the front door!" Handing me their camera, they shouldered up so I could freeze the moment.

The *Shirley* film building has the 2016 Cincinnati Toy Heritage Mural by Jonathan Queen on its western wall. In mid-March 2022, under enormous

Play-Doh can paintings, the *Shirley* film crew held their wrap party in the adjacent lot. Since the mural was painted, people love taking in this wall of Hasbro toys.

Retired toy designers sometimes bring their old work buds or families to see the work. They point and smile at the monster Strawberry Shortcake and C-3PO standing two stories high. I can't think of anything more fun and free on Court Street.

Currently on Court Street, shiny new eateries and bars have opened in the old buildings between Main and Race. The new clientele contrasts and meshes with the past.

People continue to live on Court Street: art students, library workers, and long-timers.

But beautiful older apartment houses (marble stairs, pseudo-belle epoque) are being designated for redevelopment or sold. Folks have been notified to hat up, get out, and relocate with a good-bye letter in their mail slot. Rents are too high—a lot of left-outedness in the midst. The genius loci of this neighborhood were realized long before Edison thought it was a great place to hang out. And so it will continue, I hope. I know I'll keep enjoying it until they turn the lights out.

Brighton: Memories of the Baymiller Pedestrian Bridge

JON CARTER

In 1993, I stood on the old Baymiller pedestrian bridge on the side closest to West McMicken. This bridge used to span Central Parkway between West McMicken and Central Avenue, both of which ran perpendicular to the bridge. The bridge at that time was the safest way to cross a very busy section of Central Parkway and walk up a long flight of stairs to W. McMicken just west of the bottom of Ravine Street, where the Mohawk Veterans Memorial is located.

It was early August, about 9:00 a.m., already hot, and the sun poured over the streets from the southeast in thick slices, causing bright glare on the cars that sped by. I stood there and sketched the scene of roughshod backyards facing me once I had crossed the bridge fully. Just at the base of the stairs, a ramshackle gate led to a weathered dirt path that emptied into two fairly wide backyards. Although they were not deep-set enough for children to ride bikes in, they were just right for men to sit in the cool shade and sip cold quarts of beer while playing cards.

A long flight of stairs led up to a Black-owned pony keg at the top. It sold beer, pop, cigarettes, and snacks. Most of the businesses in the West End were Black owned at this time. On the south side of Central Parkway, a nasty smelling stairwell dropped down to the upper dead end of Baymiller. People drank, puked, and urinated in the sheltered nook of the stairwell. Central Avenue crossed about forty feet down.

The old peanut factory sat adjacent to the bridge, and a slaughterhouse occupied the sole buildings in this section of Baymiller that arched gently upward to intersect Bank Street by the softball park on the corner of Baymiller. The rigged gate to those backyards was half-open.

The backyards were elevated on a high retaining wall that ran up Central Parkway about a block, culminating at the Brighton Approach. I carefully sketched this scene in detail with a pencil onto paper. A handful of disinterested people walked across the bridge from Central and on up the stairs. Then I looked it over, put it away in my sketchbook, and walked home back up Central Avenue toward the Brighton Approach. I knew at the time my painting knowledge and skills did not extend to landscape painting, and especially not to street scenes. I filed it away for use later.

I never saw anyone sitting in the backyards when I was sketching, but a dark-skinned elderly woman with red eyes spoke to me when she let a little dog out into the yard. I did see a couple of older, perhaps middle-aged men sitting in the cool shade back there on a couple of other occasions when I crossed the bridge, but I wasn't sketching them then. They laughed between guttural curses and literally chugged down a quart of beer between puffs at cigars. They nodded at me, and I waved casually as I walked by.

Many times over the coming months, I retreated to the shade that covered the stairs to West McMicken and drank ice cold beer that I'd purchased at the little store. It was a great way to while away the hours.

In 2006, I found my old sketch of the backyards on the Baymiller pedestrian bridge and did my first painting of the scene. I ineffectively covered the basics but couldn't bring it to life. It wasn't until 2018 that I was able to capture the breathtaking, impressionistic scene in all of its nuance.

Mount Adams: Life on the Hill

LIZ GOTTMER

I grew up in Mount Adams, wrapped by Eden Park on one side and downtown on the other, with so much of the Italianate architecture Cincinnati is known for, and a European vibe due to its narrow, sometimes brick-paved streets and stone walls overgrown with greenery.

Nestled on a hill overlooking downtown Cincinnati, Mount Adams is in fact nicknamed "the Hill," and shall forever be *the* Hill to me no matter how many other communities adopt the same name. Its proximity to heaven once inspired both Catholics and astronomers to build there, competing for the same high ground on which to dedicate the pursuits they each held sacred.

Ultimately, the church, and not the observatory, was to be the highest building in the city. The legend is that Archbishop Purcell, on a stormy sea voyage, prayed to Mary and promised to build a shrine to her in the most prominent and visible place in Cincinnati if she would see the ship through.

Later, as he set about fulfilling his promise, he urged the faithful of Cincinnati to undertake a "pilgrimage" to ensure its success, and thousands of Catholics wore a path in the hill to visit the site of Immaculata Church during its construction. Eventually, the path was replaced with steps, and every year on Good Friday, many continue the tradition, "praying the steps" in a ritual symbolic of Christ's climb to Golgotha.

The Holy Cross-Immaculata Parish was central to my experience growing up in Mount Adams, and its somewhat mythical history, together with the stories my parents and grandparents told about growing up there, cast my neighborhood in a sort of golden, sepia light.

I felt like I was living at the very edge of history, in a glorious place at the end of its glory days, the ordinary child of legends. I longed for my neighborhood as I had never known it to be but heard it once was—a place where everyone knew everyone, where they could always borrow a cup of sugar from the next-door neighbor, a place full of families and family-owned businesses, with enough kids at one point to populate three schools.

My sister and I are the fourth generation on both sides of our family to live in Mount Adams, but by the time we were born, you could count on two hands and maybe a foot the number of kids there. We attended St. Mary School in Hyde Park, and most of my classmates lived in the area near the school where the yards are bigger and the houses farther apart.

I loved going to their houses to play, but I wouldn't have traded living in Mount Adams for anything. We managed to have plenty of fun swinging ourselves around on the iron railing of a neighbor's front steps, climbing fences and running down "secret passageways" between houses, hanging out in the honeysuckle tree in Sarah's back garden—and after all, what backyard is better than Eden Park? Though I was vicariously nostalgic for Mount Adams's past, being one of so few kids also made it feel special, almost like a secret.

In my very own Narnia, I was surrounded by people who loved and cared about me, including all my living grandparents within two blocks of my house, and neighbors and parishioners who loved me because they loved my family.

Mine was a charmed childhood: getting ice cream at UDF with my Grandma Gottmer, or slushies from the corner store with my friend Brittany, watching old movies at my Grandma and Grandpa Lynch's, sledding down the giant hill by the old reservoir, finding the perfect spot on Oregon Street to watch the Labor Day fireworks.

Perhaps if it had been somewhat less idyllic, I wouldn't have been so naive, and I would have realized that bustling neighborhoods don't suddenly go quiet of their own accord. One factor, certainly, was the appeal to some folks of the suburbs, with more space and . . . whatever other amenities are supposed to be there. (I may have inherited my parents' not-so-subtle disdain of suburban living.)

The force that dealt the final blow, however, was several decades of unchecked development. In the 1960s, developers had begun to market Mount Adams as the ideal spot near downtown for young professionals (i.e., not "for" the blue-collar families who traditionally and still live there), and they had begun developing upscale rentals for a wealthier demographic.

My mom and dad always said that if they had left Mount Adams to start a family as many of their childhood friends had done, they wouldn't have been able to afford moving back, as their friends now couldn't.

We were only able to live in a neighborhood with higher and higher property values—despite it being where our family had lived for generations—because they had bought the house before development in Mount Adams was out of control. In a few short years, new condos and higher rents had become as rampant as the ivy choking the hill behind Holy

Cross Monastery, which is now the headquarters for one of the city's largest developers.

My grandfathers were a truck driver and a milkman, and two generations ago, Mount Adams was mostly home to working-class families. Now it belongs to folks with the disposable income to spend on "location," who can think about extra factors beyond the roof and running water.

Since the big changes on the Hill, other neighborhoods, including Over-the-Rhine, have been affected by similar waves of redevelopment. I work in that neighborhood at Peaslee Neighborhood Center, which advocates for more equitable development practices to prevent people being displaced.

While Mount Adams is no longer the community my family once knew, I am still grateful for the eighteen wonderful years I spent there—and that it led me to the work I do now, trying to keep its story from being repeated again and again.

UPTOWN

Avondale: It Takes a Village

DEQAH HUSSEIN-WETZEL

Sandra Jones-Mitchell remembers the long years where it seemed like no one wanted to invest in Avondale, the neighborhood where she grew up and where she currently serves as community council president.

It "feels that Avondale has had a For Sale sign on it for the last twenty years," she says.

It was a For Sale sign that brought her family here in the 1970s as they sought to escape the crowded environs of Cumminsville, a Cincinnati neighborhood just north of the central city. In Avondale, that For Sale sign sat outside an affordable two-family home with a yard—something Jones-Mitchell's family, along with so many other Black families at the time, fought through redlining and blatant market-based housing discrimination to attain.

Jones-Mitchell and her family found themselves in the auto-centric urban center of Avondale. The main thoroughfare, Reading Road, seemed ten lanes wide. She could no longer walk to school, that was for certain.

This was just a few years after the civil unrest in 1967 and 1968 that tore through Avondale.

"A lot of the buildings were still there on Reading Road," she says. "It was still boarded up. There were no stores, it was a few bars, and even the Kroger was closing."

And to make matters worse, some of the buildings that had burned down hadn't been torn down yet.

Already, middle-class white families had been fleeing Avondale for over two decades. Attributed to white flight, between 1950 and 1960, the white population dropped from about 21,000 to just under 9,000, while the Black population soared from almost 3,500 to nearly 20,000.

With the demographic changes came disinvestment. And things got worse after the 1967 riots.

Similar to many neighborhoods in urban areas across the country, civil unrest in the late 1960s was omnipresent and destructive.

In the short term, the uprisings in Cincinnati, which started as a protest in June of 1967, resulted in the police arresting over 200 people, and property damage totaling $3 million ($22 million today).

The unrest devastated Avondale physically and socially—people were hurt, storefront windows were shattered, and the National Guard was called in to contain the Black folks who were rightfully pissed off that their neighborhood had been neglected since white flight.

Not only did the swift white exodus in Avondale create an uphill battle for low- and moderate-income African Americans to build their community away from Cincinnati's previous center of Black life in the West End, in the long term, the upwelling of anger engendered decades of economic and social disinvestment.

Like Jones-Mitchell, Jan Michele Lemon Kearney has spent her life in Avondale. Now a Cincinnati city councilmember, Lemon Kearney remembers that time.

"There were some neighbors down the street who sat on their front porch and watched," she says. "The idea was like, the people out in the streets are fighting for us, you know, they're fighting for all of us. People had just been through a lot."

As the decades wore on, investment slowly began trickling, then flooding, back into Avondale. But there's a funny thing about investment—it's not always an entirely benevolent force.

Back when Avondale was shifting in the 1950s and 1960s, Jewish hospitals and the central business district lined Burnett Avenue. Today, most of these buildings have been demolished to allow for the expansion of University of Cincinnati hospitals and medical buildings.

"They did encroach on the neighborhood," Lemon Kearney says. And she's not just talking about the hospital expansion. She's calling out the Cincinnati Zoo, too.

"There was a playground right across the street that had a basketball court—all the neighborhood would play there. But in the 1990s, the zoo took over that playground and made it into a parking lot. This was a really unfortunate time in the history of zoo-Avondale relations."

Lemon Kearney recalls her dad walking a picket line, protesting the zoo over that playground while she was in law school.

Luckily, the relationship Avondale has with the hospital and zoo is much better than what it used to be.

"One of the things that makes our community councils strong is when the relationship that you have with the institutions are strong," Jones-Mitchell says. "And I can say today that relationship is a lot better than it was. It's going to take a village to make Avondale grow. . . . I encourage it at every meeting that we allow the residents to be a little bit more engaged."

The business district in Avondale has shifted from Burnet Avenue to Reading Road, and today, the latter arterial street connects the neighborhood to the rest of the city. It is even busier and more congested than it was when Jones-Mitchell first gazed upon it as a child in the 1970s.

In 2017, the MLK interchange, a new exit off I-71, opened up near Reading Road to serve as a gateway to the hospitals on Burnet Avenue. Over time, the improved transportation corridor paved the way for development to come into the neighborhood, which includes the University of Cincinnati's Innovation Corridor.

To combat too much institutional expansion, however, the neighborhood is supported by the Avondale Community Council, the Avondale Development Corporation, and the Avondale Business Association, who all work together to make sure residents' voices are heard.

It's because of this community participation that Jones-Mitchell is so hopeful for the future.

"I am a believer that nothing should happen in Avondale without us, and we need to be at the table, and we need to be able to help folks decide what we want," she says. "I'm going to be a voice because not only do I have property here, I have family here. I lived here. It's our community. And I'm going to stand on that."

North Avondale: Satisfaction in the Effort

JULIE ZIMMERMAN

Like most North Avondale residents, we first fell in love with the house.

It had an imposing red-brick façade that was three stories high, trimmed in an unfortunate yellow and brown, with a deep front porch covered in artificial grass. Behind the massive wood door lay a staircase of quarter-sawn oak that had once been painted white and was now half-stripped. The original chandelier of brass and stained glass had also been painted; the tile and mirror on the handsome living-room fireplace were an incongruous baby blue. Sprinkled throughout, though, were swoon-worthy features: a dining room of unpainted judge's paneling, built-ins, and a beamed ceiling in the same quarter-sawn oak; a stained-glass window spanning a floor and a half in the front stairway; a third-floor family room with six walk-in closets.

The house needed us. And so, two months before our wedding, we bypassed the search for a starter home and went straight to the house we'd eventually raise our family in. Over the next decades, we coaxed it back to something resembling its original grandeur: the textured ceilings were smoothed, wood floors refinished, chandelier and light fixtures stripped and polished, and kitchen and baths renovated. We raised two children, hosted parties, gardened, and built a wonderful life in a house we loved.

After we'd moved in, though, we realized we'd become not just caretakers of a house but also of a neighborhood, one where nearly everyone felt a responsibility for its preservation. North Avondale isn't well known within the city or the region; when we opened our front door, most first-time visitors exclaimed, "I never knew this neighborhood was back here!" But behind the scenes, there were countless residents dedicated to keeping the neighborhood vibrant.

North Avondale was developed in the late nineteenth century, built as a residential subdivision with winding streets and homes situated on large lots with ample lawns. Merchants and manufacturers such as Barney Kroger, Samuel Pogue, and Andrew Erkenbrecher built mansions in the neighborhood; one has a sense, moving through its streets, that an arms race of social competition propelled their construction, yielding a textbook of grand architectural styles.

It continued as a prosperous neighborhood for the first half of the twentieth century, with its defining moment arriving around 1960. As displacement of downtown residents led Black families to move north from the urban core to areas such as Avondale, Evanston, Bond Hill, and Roselawn, white families, panicked by racist real estate tactics and their own fears, fled to newly developed suburbs, taking resources with them and leaving empty churches and schools behind. The rapid changes and falling real estate values destabilized many communities, as did the haphazard division of larger homes into multifamily units.

In 1960, residents of North Avondale came together to form the North Avondale Neighborhood Association, hoping to halt white flight and preserve racial and economic integration. When we moved into North Avondale, we met neighbors of all races who had lived through the tumultuous 1960s and 1970s, when friends and family urged them to get out or move somewhere else. Some had been involved in the effort to desegregate the neighborhood's Clinton Hills Swim Club, which became the first racially integrated pool in the city. All who remained had resisted the fear of what might happen to them personally in favor of solidarity with a community they loved.

As we settled into North Avondale, I began to notice the many ways that residents worked on behalf of the neighborhood: showing up at the monthly NANA meetings and clean-up days, writing grant applications for Reading Road improvements, testifying before the city's planning commission on various projects, running for public office. In a city of fifty-two neighborhoods, there's nearly always one of the nine city council members who lives in North Avondale, and often two or three: Jan-Michele Lemon Kearney, Christopher Smitherman, Wendell Young, Cecil Thomas, Bobbie Sterne, Minette Cooper, and Jeanette Cissell to name a few, along with numerous Cincinnati school board members, state senators, and others.

At times, living in a neighborhood like North Avondale can seem like a lot of work, with neighbors who are unusually vigilant and suspicious of any changes. On her daily walks, one neighbor used to look for extra electric meters or other signs that a property had been illegally divided into multiple units. Another time, I attended a NANA meeting after Xavier University had offered to develop public land along Victory Parkway into tennis courts and walking trails for the university and the public to use. It seemed like a no-brainer to me, but longtime residents who had found disappointment behind big promises before questioned why the city couldn't develop the land itself. (Xavier eventually developed the courts minus the lights in the original plan, which were deemed a potential nuisance to neighbors.)

Living in a racially integrated neighborhood has taught me things I hadn't learned in the majority-white places I'd lived before. It's encouraging to know that, with effort and attention, a neighborhood can remain racially and economically diverse for decades. At the same time, it's discouraging to encounter people who assume that the neighborhood is unsafe because of its demographics and location. For every handful of visitors who told us they'd never known about North Avondale before, there was one who blurted out, "Aren't you afraid to live here?" at our front door. It took a while and a little bit of practice for me to offer a puzzled look and say, "What exactly do you mean?" to underscore the racism at the heart of the question. At summertime swim meets, there were painful "jokes" from other teams about whether it was safe to park their cars in the area. One sitter we (briefly) employed refused to let our kids play outside because she didn't think it was safe. While neighbors develop a gallows humor about incidents like these, hearing such sentiments shared aloud is a powerful reminder of the casual racism running underneath so many interactions.

We celebrated twenty-five years in our house this spring, morphing in what seems like no time from newcomers to old-timers. Our house, which has felt like a fixer-upper for most of the time we've lived in it, finally feels close to finished, as much as any old house is ever finished. Home values in the neighborhood have spiked since the onset of the pandemic, as they have nearly everywhere, leading to fears that the diversity at the heart of the community's identity may now be threatened.

I think North Avondale will find a way to preserve its character in the face of prosperity, just as it's overcome other challenges over the decades. There are easier places to live than a neighborhood like North Avondale, places where you can drive into the garage at night, slip in the back door, and forget about the world outside. Places that ask little of their residents except that they pay their taxes and mow their grass. But places that ask nothing of their residents give very little in return. Things of value require care and effort to preserve. And so often, it's in the effort itself—the elbow grease, the late-night volunteer emails, the small victories and incremental improvements of both house and community—where that satisfaction resides.

Clifton: "That's Not Clifton"

ANNE SKOVE

My seventh-grade history teacher once explained the federal deficit by invoking the popular eighties bogey(wo)man: "If single mothers living DOWNTOWN and in CLIFTON would just get jobs, the government wouldn't have to support them!"

Born and raised in Clifton by a single mom, I spent that year at a private school in Indian Hill on scholarship. My mom wasn't working. She joked, "We could be on welfare!" She described our kitchen, with its fire-sale green and brown carpet over broken linoleum, as "inner city."

Was my history teacher talking about *my* mom and my neighborhood? This was the first time I wanted to say, "That's not Clifton."

I didn't know any welfare queens, not in my neighborhood or elsewhere. He didn't have to, and didn't, say the word "Black." But it was clear what the assumption was.

Mine was the second bus stop on the way to school each morning. First stop: Mount Airy, two Black kids, single mom. Second stop: me, one white kid, adopted by a single mom. Third stop: Avondale, two more Black kids, single mom. Then, a long all-white haul to the richest parts of Hyde Park, Mount Lookout, and eastward. Many of the wealthy kids had extended stepfamilies, but nobody talked about their neighborhoods.

Clifton, where I was born and raised, was incorporated as a lush suburban village in the 1850s and named after a 1,200-acre farm on the site of the current neighborhood. Its pastoral past is still visible in McMansions of yesteryear on estate-sized plots in the neighborhood's far northern reaches. A respite from the frantic, sooty city below, Clifton's well-to-do residents cultivated a serene, park-like atmosphere. You can still catch that vibe in Burnet Woods, the eighty-nine-acre park that extends to Clifton's southeast corner.

Cincinnati annexed Clifton in 1893, and the University of Cincinnati occupied an insanely large portion of Burnet Woods outside the neighborhood soon after. Ever since, people have been mixed up about what, exactly, is and isn't Clifton.

Suburbanites and the media get confused. When local television news reported that a protest for racial justice broke windows at a Subway restaurant in Clifton, I was surprised I hadn't heard any noise, as there is a

Subway nearby. They meant the Subway by the University of Cincinnati. That's not Clifton.

For many, their primary encounter with the area is often the University of Cincinnati, which is just south of Clifton proper. UC spreads out over Clifton, abutting neighborhoods that at one time or another were known as Clifton Heights, Fairview, University Heights, Uptown, Corryville, or CUF.

Soon after we moved back to my hometown, my husband encountered these beliefs. "We live in Clifton, in the house my wife grew up in," he told a guy. The guy, who probably was last in the city for a Reagan-era frat party, responded, "I didn't realize it had a residential area."

Realtors market rentals as "Clifton." Clifton was once affordable enough for professors and students. Back in the day, two of the eight houses on my street, plus two across the alley behind us, belonged to fraternities. My mom moved here to teach at UC. One of UC's top chemistry professors lived on our street. I can hear the school's homecoming parade from our house. While I spend most of my days in the shadow of UC's gargantuan Crosley Building, that's not Clifton.

Fairview, a public school that concentrates on German, was originally in Fairview. *Das ist nicht Klifton.* The old Fairview building became beautiful condos. The current site is that of the 1970s-era Clifton School, across the street from the original Clifton Elementary School building (now Clifton Area Neighborhood School, or CANS). The German school still has "Fairview" in its name. The current location is in Clifton. I guess they didn't want to confuse anybody.

Sometimes, our own snobbery is at work. Newer homeowners may need to justify the large sums they paid for their houses in Clifton's 45220 zip code. If local news erroneously reports a crime location, "that's not Clifton." We are safe under the fuzzy yellow glow of our ancient gaslights.

Which brings us to "gaslight district," a term used by realtors to explain that they really, *really* mean the property is in Clifton this time. Hence, Gaslight Property, Gaslight Apartments, and the late Gaslight Gourmet Cookies and GJ's Gaslight (no relation to the new Gaslight Bar and Grill).

There are gaslights on side streets, but also, intermittently, newfangled electric lights. Although the Esquire Theater on Clifton's main drag, Ludlow Avenue, finally showed the film *Gaslight*, marketers learned nothing from Angela Lansbury. Or maybe they're gaslighting us.

Other manufactured names nearby include "CUF" and "Uptown." "CUF" refers to Clifton Heights, University Heights, and Fairview. The acronym takes up less space than "near UC." Given the hilly effects of the city's glacial history, "Uptown" could be anywhere, except the non-hilly riverside. By fate, it seems to be part of the area atop Vine Street hill, excluding Mount Auburn.

In any event, neither CUF nor Uptown are Clifton. They might more accurately be called "That's Not Clifton."

Clifton Market, on Ludlow where Keller's IGA used to be, is in Clifton. The business district along Ludlow, which intersects with Clifton Avenue, is called "Clifton." That's Clifton, although Clifton Avenue is so long that much of it is not. If you say, "I'm going up to Clifton," when you are clearly in the neighborhood, you mean, "I'm going up to Ludlow." I once knew a woman who had lived here all her life. If she were going to Keller's, she would say, "I'm going to town." That's Clifton.

However, the so-called Clifton Mini Mart, at McMillan and Highland in Mount Auburn, is not. Perhaps they named it to reflect the spirit of Clifton. This was the case for Chicago Gyros, which is obviously not in Chicago, but rather (possibly) CUF. But unless the Clifton Mini Mart sells handmade ceramic hookahs, features local art on their walls, doubles as a notary, allows dogs, and caters to at least four eccentric regulars a day, they are not Cliftonesque.

Proctor & Gamble used to provide employees with a list of places not to live. Clifton was on that list. Now, Clifton is acceptable. Both of these are the same Clifton.

Even when you're safely within the borders of Clifton proper, the complexity remains.

"NELA," an acronym used on Google Groups by people hosting porch parties, means "North East of Ludlow Avenue," my part of the world. When my friend moved to the Tudor Apartments on Ludlow, he felt he'd moved away. NELA is "gaslight," but many old-school Cliftonites live here.

Before NELA, Bi-We-Hos-Ox was an annual picnic named for NELA streets Bishop, Wentworth, Hosea, and Oxford Terrace. It's all Clifton, except for some Bishop Street houses that originally faced Ruther, which is only Clifton on that side of the street. The west side of Ruther? That's not Clifton.

Is "That's not Clifton" suburban racism or local pride? Poor map skills or very exacting ones? My seventh-grade teacher saw parts of the city as one homogeneous welfare state, ruled by lazy queens. Today, the Twitter account @thatsnotclifton includes a link to an official (?) map. Its mission is "Doing yeoman's work to educate the uneducated," quite a goal for a Twitter account, or anyone.

Burnet Woods: Ducks on a Pond

ANNE DELANO STEINERT

Some weekend mornings when I was a kid, my dad would make us pancakes. He would make more than we could eat so we could walk to Burnet Woods to feed the extras to the ducks.

Ducks on a pond only a few minutes' walk from my house were just one of the childhood wonders the woods provided. The park gave me safe places to take the kinds of risks kids need to grow up; I both loved and feared the stone slide, and I climbed rocks, waded through the lake's drainage tunnel, and explored the cool wooded paths just like Laura Ingalls in her big woods. Once a 170-acre plot of native woods and bluegrass, the municipal park is still a Cincinnati treasure and a trove of history, nature, and beauty.

Burnet Woods was so named long before it became a city park and a university campus. In May 1871, an ad in the *Cincinnati Enquirer* offered lots in "the well known Burnet Woods" at auction. If this "Great Sale of Beautiful Lots in Burnet's Subdivision" had gone forward, Cincinnati would have grown up without two of the city's richest resources.

By 1871, Burnet Woods, once owned by Senator Jacob Burnet, belonged to his children, Robert Wallace Burnet and Elizabeth Burnet Groesbeck (I get annoyed that most accounts say the land was sold to the city by Robert Burnet and William Groesbeck when in fact, Elizabeth, Groesbeck's wife, was the co-owner). Apparently, there had been talk of converting the woods into a city park for years. The advertised auction was probably an attempt to move the park proposal along, and just four months later, the park board discussed an offer to rent the land (the upper sixty acres of which were described as "native woods") for ninety-nine years.

The original park stretched from 100 feet north of Calhoun Street to Ludlow Avenue. Today, more than half of that land is the campus of the University of Cincinnati, separated from the remaining wooded park by the eight-lane Martin Luther King Drive.

Burnet Woods is an urban oasis, laced with hiking trails and dotted with landmarks. The most obvious feature is a stocked fishing pond edged by an ornamented bridge. When I was a kid, there were paddle boats for rent and a place to buy food for the ducks. White ducks used to live here year-round, but global warming or urban pollution has sent them packing, and now it's exciting to see ducks stopping off even for a few days. I have a friend who calls or texts when there are ducks in the pond, but it's not very often. West of the lake is a gorgeous carved stone bridge with incised ornaments reminiscent of New York's Central Park.

Across the street from the pond is the Trailside Nature Center, built by the Works Progress Administration (WPA) of FDR's New Deal in 1939. The building has been altered over the years, but it still clearly combines natural materials, like rough cut stone and whole logs, with streamlined design and modern steel and glass. An historic photo of the building shows its original flat roof looking like a design directly off Frank Lloyd Wright's drawing board—though the real architect was the park board's own Carl Freund. The building holds teaching collections of plants and animals and a planetarium where the roof cranks open to the night sky.

Next to the Trailside Nature Center is my favorite part of the park, the aforementioned concrete slide built by the WPA in 1940. This one you have to experience to appreciate, but my best tip for success is to bring a large piece of cardboard to sit on. If you want to go faster, you can wrap the cardboard in wax paper.

Once you've shredded your pants on the slide and poked around the nature center, walk toward UC's campus. On your way, you might pass a stack of architectural salvage on the hillside. These carved stone pieces were salvaged from the Cincinnati Chamber of Commerce Building, which burned down in 1911. The imposing building stood at Fourth and Vine Streets, where the PNC tower is today, Cincinnati's only building by American architect Henry Hobson Richardson (father of the Richardson Romanesque style). The stones were saved by the Cincinnati Astronomical Society, which planned to use them in a new building. The society never realized their plans, and in 1969, a UC professor found the pieces warehoused in Cleves and worked with his students to create what is sometimes called "Cincinnati Stonehenge."

On the other side of Martin Luther King lies "The Burnet Woods Campus" of the University of Cincinnati. UC first took a little nibble out of the park for McMicken Hall (the old one, not the one we have today, which was built in 1950) and then Van Wormer, but over time, it took bigger and bigger bites. Now the hilly terrain is all that remains of that original park.

UC's first campus was located on founding donor Charles McMicken's estate on the hillside at the top of Elm Street. In his will, McMicken stated his intention to establish a college for "white boys and girls" on his land, but it turned out to be a very bad place for a college. The noise of the nearby incline, the sooty city air, and the sloping hillside made it inhospitable to both scholarly and social activity, and after twenty years, university trustees petitioned the city to move into Burnet Woods. (It is worth noting that they ignored McMicken's racism and granted a degree to African American William Parham in 1874, just four years after opening their doors on McMicken's hillside).

When I look at the 1884 *Robinson Atlas*, I see Burnet Woods extending all the way south to Calhoun Street, and I mourn the massive urban park it once was, but as an alumna of the University of Cincinnati, I am grateful for the education I received on the Burnets' land, and because my parents met at UC, I'm indebted to it for my very existence. The original McMicken Hall opened in Burnet Woods in 1895, marking the beginning of the university's takeover of the park. Though the initial transfer of land to UC promised that the public would not be excluded from the park around the university buildings, today's UC is a dense urban campus, notoriously remote for most Cincinnatians.

Though the campus expanded slowly at first, there is a student-drawn image in the 1915 *Cincinnatian* yearbook featuring a jolly Charles McMicken cradling his brand-new building babies. Captioned "Father McMicken," the image shows five new university buildings. From there, the campus filled the lower portion of the park, taking even more parkland in 1950. UC's campus now boasts 119 buildings serving about 46,000 students on four campuses.

Jacob Burnet and Charles McMicken both died in the 1850s in an industrializing Cincinnati that was drastically different from the one we know now. They couldn't have imagined Cincinnati or UC or Burnet Woods today. But here is McMicken's university in Burnet's woods, providing us with spaces to relax, reflect, rejuvenate, explore, and learn—I just wish there were still ducks.

Mount Auburn: On Rice Street

NICK SWARTSELL

Many Cincinnatians will never drive down Rice Street in Mount Auburn.

From its start at Mulberry Street just north of Over-the-Rhine, the tucked-away street passes a few blocks of modest two-story houses. Then it makes an S-curve, passing the sheer, rocky cliff that holds up Christ Hospital's parking garage on one side and a small, calm playground bordered by a dense clump of trees on the other.

After the curves, there are two more blocks of houses.

Samuel DuBose died here almost six years ago, in the spot before Rice makes a tight turn to become Thill Street, which runs to Vine Street. An occasionally changing memorial marked by candles, a faded T-shirt with his image, and sometimes deflated balloons attached to a telephone pole still mark the spot at the corner of Valencia Street where the unarmed Black motorist's Honda Accord stopped after he was shot in the head by a white University of Cincinnati police officer, Ray Tensing, during a routine traffic stop.

But Rice Street is more than just the place where DuBose was killed.

In the years after the national news cameras and police tape, after the memorial balloons, Rice Street still passes through a community full of neighbors, parents, and children—younger and longtime residents. Like many neighborhoods that have seen controversial police shootings, both in Cincinnati and across the country, the census tract where DuBose died is one of its city's poorest.

It is quiet here most days. The sounds of birds mix with the hovering hum of Christ Hospital's massive climate control equipment, which looms on the hill above.

Residents are friendly, though some don't like to be quoted in articles. Many will tell you all about their community, though.

Rosemary Carr moved onto Valencia Street in 1986.

"I love it," she said of the neighborhood, which she didn't want defined by the shooting that happened five houses down from her. "I just love Mount Auburn."

DuBose, who lived in Avondale, was driving near UC's campus when Tensing noticed he didn't have a front license plate. Tensing followed

DuBose, pulling him over just under a mile away from campus. There, after a few minutes of arguing with DuBose after he failed to produce a driver's license, Tensing shot the father of thirteen in the head.

Tensing originally told other officers that DuBose dragged him with his car before he fired. But body camera footage seems to show Tensing firing on DuBose without cause while DuBose's car was stationary. Two juries in Hamilton County could not agree to convict him.

Carr said she's never heard a satisfactory explanation for why the UC officer was there in the first place. She's angry that DuBose was killed.

Some of her neighbors, including Charna Corbin, who lived a few houses down, were similarly distraught about DuBose's death and suggested naming the street after him. Corbin said she'd like to get a petition going. But Carr balked at that.

"Him getting shot here didn't have anything to do with the neighborhood," she said. "It had to do with the police."

In one way, Carr is right—that DuBose's death happened at this isolated corner of Cincinnati was a matter of circumstance. But the neighborhood has a lot in common with many other neighborhoods where law enforcement intertwines with poverty and racial issues—including those in cities like Baltimore, Ferguson, Missouri, Chicago, and here in Cincinnati—and that have seen controversial police shootings.

Rice Street runs down the middle of much of the city's census tract twenty-three, a small area that stretches from McMillan Avenue at the north end, along Vine and Mulberry Streets to the west and south, and along Auburn Avenue and Sycamore Street to the east.

Three-quarters of the tract's 1,143 residents are Black. The median household income here is $16,344—half the city's overall median. Three-hundred-fifty-four of the tract's 810 housing units sit vacant. Sixty-five percent of its residents pay more than 40 percent of their income for rent; 56 percent pay half or more of their income for rent.

Despite sitting in the shadow of one of the state's biggest public universities, only 13 percent of residents in census tract twenty-three have a bachelor's degree. And though one of the city's premier hospitals sits in the middle of the area, life expectancy in Mount Auburn is three years below the average for the city.

When Carr moved in three decades ago, her street ran up to a dense section of row houses that surrounded Glencoe Place. That development, first built in the late 1800s, saw alternating fortunes over the years. By the 1950s, city officials considered it a slum. A 1970s redevelopment as middle-class housing won national urban planning awards, but by the mid-1990s, it was vacant.

Then Glencoe Place was blocked off to through traffic, sealing off Valencia Street from a busy neighborhood artery, Auburn Avenue. The row houses were demolished in 2013. Today, the area seems to be reverting to a kind of urban prairie, concrete cracking and weeds growing in the blocks that once held hundreds of people.

The vacant blocks of Glencoe and the occasional empty houses make the area around Rice Street feel isolated, though residents there said they love the quiet, the greenness, and the tight-knit feeling.

But they said more could be done for them and for their children.

"We need things for the kids to do around here, positive things," Carr said, noting that young people in the area need activities that will keep them out of danger.

Following DuBose's death, UCPD temporarily stopped, for the most part, patrolling in the neighborhoods off campus after it was ordered to do so by the city of Cincinnati. But why was UCPD in neighborhoods like Mount Auburn in the first place?

UCPD's role in the neighborhoods surrounding campus dates back to an agreement between the department and Cincinnati police signed in 1989. S. Gregory Baker, UCPD director of police community relations, says the university ramped up its police force in the years preceding the DuBose shooting in response to a spike in crime around the university that started around 2008. The school ended up doubling the thirty-five officers it had in 2013 to seventy in just a year and a half. By 2016, it was the third-largest law enforcement agency in Hamilton County behind the Cincinnati Police Department and the Hamilton County Sheriff's Office.

UCPD presence in surrounding neighborhoods was boosted when UC hired former Lamar University police chief Jason Goodrich to lead the department.

Traffic stops went up 300 percent in 2015 under Goodrich's tenure. Arrests also tripled. With that surge, racial disparities also increased. During this time, stops of white individuals actually decreased. Black stops went way up, however.

Neighborhoods like Mount Auburn "were, according to the chief, to be effectively 'no fly zones,' through which, via excessive traffic enforcement, criminals would not want to drive," a report on the department by an outside company called Exiger reads.

Tensing seems to have exemplified this more aggressive approach during his time at UCPD, stopping and arresting far more suspects than the average UC cop.

Four out of five traffic tickets Tensing issued were against Black motorists, and three-quarters of arrests were of Blacks. In the same time frame, UCPD officers as a whole gave more than 60 percent of their tickets to Black motorists.

"Was it racist?" Baker once asked about those disparities at a police-community relations panel. "If it walks like a duck and talks like a duck..."

Residents suggest that level of policing might not be necessary.

Eba Erco, who moved into the neighborhood on Rice Street about six months after Tensing shot DuBose, says he liked it there because it was calm. Erco, who had recently graduated from UC at the time he moved in, says he could "kind of understand" the presence of UC police on his old street, Wheeler, which is much closer to campus and where there were a number of break-ins and muggings. But in this quiet cove? He doesn't see why a university officer would be there.

A heat map of Cincinnati Police Department data shows the areas around Rice, Valencia, and neighboring streets in a deep shade of blue—meaning a low number of incidents—next to orange and red splotches that signify higher levels on nearby Vine Street to the west and McMillan Avenue to the north. The year before DuBose was killed saw only a couple small incidents there, including a person breaking into a vacant house and the theft of six dollars from a woman's wallet. There is one exception—a murder that happened on Gage Street to the south in the weeks after DuBose's death—but otherwise, the area is much less active than others to the north, closer to UC, or further south into Over-the-Rhine.

As conversations about policing in working-class and Black neighborhoods continue to be heated, residents on Rice Street and its surroundings waited for more concrete improvements to their neighborhood.

Carr said she was focused on a park just north of her street. As she spoke, her half-dozen elementary- and middle-school-aged grandchildren filed out her front door to meet their mother.

Inwood Park used to have more amenities where kids could go play, she said, making it a spot for people in the neighborhood to congregate in a positive way. But Carr said the park had become neglected, crime had gone up, and playing there had gotten more dangerous. The Cincinnati City Council mulled money for a rehab of the park the year DuBose died, but it was left out of the city's budget.

Carr said she's hopeful the memorial on the corner near her house will come down some day. She was glad it was there for the first few months. But now it is fading, decaying.

"I'm ready to move on," she said. "Why remind yourself of something tragic that way?"

WEST

The Mill Creek Valley: Illuminating Obstacles

ELISSA YANCEY

It's been close to a decade since I first stepped foot in Cincinnati's Mill Creek. Close to a decade since I first heard the word "portage" and came to understand its meaning in an up-close-and-personal, leaky-boots-squishy way.

Portage is the act of carrying a boat (or in my case, a canoe) from one body of water to another to avoid obstacles. In my first trip on the Mill Creek—part small urban river, part civil engineering project—in early 2013, I had more than forty chances to "portage" my canoe along three miles.

In those days, that stretch of the Mill Creek was an obstacle course of empty bottles, discarded plastic containers, and slime-covered rocks. It wasn't a pleasant haul, but I was lucky to be part of a lively guided tour led by a few rowdy renegade members of the sassily named "Mill Creek Yacht Club," a volunteer group of pioneer-like nature-lovers dedicated to the health and well-being of the twenty-eight-mile creek.

I was hooked. Within a year, I had taken at least three more canoe trips along the Mill Creek, both as an environmental journalist and as a professor leading a field trip of college environmental journalism students.

Two times I put in at West Chester Township and ended at Twin Creek Preserve, marveling at the chainsaw-wielding yacht-clubbers intent on clearing gnarly log jams and loading their canoes with dumped tires and broken shopping carts. Once, I took a nighttime paddle through the industry-lined creek section through Northside and southward. Views of the glowing factories pumping plumes into the inky sky, like a postapocalyptic Instagram filter, mixed with an eerie quiet that was disrupted only by the hum of I-75 above us and the deep mechanical breaths of third-shift life.

No two trips were ever the same, and no matter how experienced the guide, there were always unpredictable and sometimes terrifying portages—during the field trip, adventurous students had to help carry all of our canoes over a mound of garbage that straddled the creek like a dam, reaching more than twenty feet high.

Still, during every trip, I marveled at the history that flows with the Mill Creek: it connects forty Cincinnati neighborhoods and thirty-seven political jurisdictions, including my hometown of Norwood, before ending in the Ohio River.

The Ohio, where ports like Cincinnati helped build the country's industrial growth, and which has long held the title of most polluted river in the country. In trip after trip, I was brought up short by how the very concept of portage—finding ways to overcome obstacles—is itself an apt symbol for the much-maligned, city-shaping creek.

The very thing that made the Mill Creek so valuable has also been what imperiled its future: it offered a clear path, rich with life and life-sustaining resources, to connect people with what they needed to survive.

Indigenous people like the Shawnee understood the value of the creek, which they called Maketewah, as its wildlife and water nourished their villages nearby. White settlers branching out from Cincinnati's riverfront clumsily followed suit, setting up homesteads along the creek. Businesses and industries—slaughterhouses, breweries, and a well-known soap factory, for starters—came next, using free and easy access to water to build and transport their goods, as well as their sewage.

As Cincinnati grew, the Mill Creek bore the refuse of more than just the industries along its banks: the city's early household waste system still feeds into a combined sewer overflow, an engineering fail-safe against flooding that combines raw sewage with rain and routes the nasty bouillabaisse into the creek and, ultimately, the mighty, muddy Ohio.

In 2013, I asked a Metropolitan Sewer District engineer for a reference point as to just how much sewage overflow entered the Mill Creek every year. How much sewage comes from just one of the concrete tunnels constructed by the Army Corps of Engineers in the 1980s, the infamous Combined Sewer Overflow (CSO) 005? The giant tunnel sits at the edge of the industrial neighborhood of South Fairmount, one of several neighborhoods that has borne the brunt of deindustrialization and disinvestment in Cincinnati.

Would the amount of sewage flowing from that pipe every year fill Paul Brown Stadium downtown, I wondered? After doing calculations involving bowl dimensions, gallons, and a kind of higher-order math I only vaguely understand, he sent me his answer: CSO 005 releases enough overflow annually to fill Paul Brown Stadium three times.

That answer came more than four decades after the passage of the federal Clean Water Act in 1972. It came more than two decades after the Environmental Protection Agency published its first-ever comprehensive analysis of the creek. That ninety-seven-page, 1992 report noted, among other things, that creek water still regularly turned red and green along

"Bloody Run," a 2,200-acre watershed in Hamilton County.

The report came fifteen years after American Waterways named the Mill Creek the country's most endangered waterway in 1997, a designation that, the work of the Yacht Club and passionate coalitions of creek-adjacent communities notwithstanding, helped elevate public conversations—and action—geared toward removing toxic obstacles that threatened the Mill Creek's future.

Obstacles like those that have plagued the Mill Creek for generations don't disappear quickly or cheaply. Still, progress in the past eight years has brought renewed life, and depth, to stretches of the Mill Creek where I once struggled to hold up my half of a canoe. A glimpse of an active beaver dam on a restored creek bank. A blue heron perched on a concrete slab of a waterway near the entrance to a foliage-lined feeder bed. A giant turtle poking its head from a tree branch half-immersed in water where fish swim quickly beneath the surface.

Perhaps man-made obstacles are never a match for the inevitability of nature, but the current life of the Mill Creek gives me hope for a more mutual kind of survival story. It's a survival story rooted in appreciation of both nature and nurture, of interdependence and appreciation. It's a story that recognizes that overcoming obstacles, no matter their source, requires strength, determination, and an ability to wade through unknown waters in search of a smoother route forward.

Camp Washington: An Island in the Stream

JOCELYN GIBSON

When we moved into our home in Camp Washington in 2019, a metal nub of gaslight piping was protruding from the living room ceiling. It was wrapped in black duct tape that we had to peel back. It was unattractive but stirring. Just like the coal chute in the basement, there is something about seeing the evidence of the conventions of past life that reminds you of your place in time.

We have learned the story of our neighborhood in pieces, bit by bit—industrial history, military history, and stories about the people who lived and worked within feet of our doorstep throughout Camp Washington's existence.

It has never been a neighborhood where one goes to enjoy natural settings or fresh air; it is housing mixed with heavy and light industry. It was settled as an army barracks during the Mexican-American war. It has an energy—of making and toiling—compounded by the fact that it is an island bounded on each side by a vast rail yard and one of the busiest interstate highways in the United States. Even if you wanted to engage in quiet leisure here, you'd be hard pressed to find a venue to entertain it. The largest park in the neighborhood is the site of the former Cincinnati Workhouse.

Having said all of this, one might wonder about the appeal of living here, and I will point to the making and toiling. You can leave your house every day as a worker or maker, in whatever form that entails, and come as you are into the daylight. That appeals to a certain kind of person, and they have congregated here on this carbon-fumed island. There is a diversity and sense of community that I hope is not fleeting in the age of supercharged urban land speculation.

From the 1880s to the mid-nineteenth century, it was a center of production. In the great flood of 1937, the floodwaters famously caught fire in Camp Washington. The homes here were generally built in the late 1800s; most still contain the impeccable craftsmanship imported by the Cincinnati immigrants and traveling laborers of the time. Into the late fifties, the neighborhood's 12,000 residents found employment, raucous taverns, bakeries, groceries, two schools, and restaurants that served "plate lunches" to the workers.

I-75 needed to go somewhere, and it was constructed through historic city neighborhoods with working-class and low-income residents, including Camp Washington. It is a demarcation point for Camp Washington residents who remember this neighborhood fabric pre- and post-federal highway construction.

A population of 12,000 slowly transformed into a population of 1,300, leaving vacant housing and storefronts in the following decades. It's true that American cities were seeing declining populations, but for the residents of Camp Washington, the highway construction was a transition point compounded by the loss of industry.

When John and Karen Volz moved to Camp Washington in 1973, they were looking for an affordable place to rent. At $65 a month, they were sold. They bought the house they rented on Bates Avenue through a land contract a few years later with intentions to flip it. But several children and Catholic school tuition meant those intentions of flipping became staying put.

Camp Washington became home, and fifty years later, they are still here. Karen was an office "Girl Friday"—an old term for female office staff. John was a full-time musician at the Ramada Inn in northern Kentucky, and they were both in a regionally successful music group called Street Corner Symphony. As musicians, they gained popularity as a talented opening act for artists like Frankie Valli, Gene Chandler, and the famed Pittsburgh doo-wop group the Skyliners.

They won't tell you about their place in Cincinnati music history unless you catch them on a social evening—the stories are great, and the recordings of their music are even better. A capella and doo-wop music is their genre; perfect alto and soprano pitches from their performing days rise out of the jukebox in their living room.

Their recollections of the neighborhood are colorful and include prison guards from the workhouse running through their backyard with pump rifles, chasing wayward prisoners, though without a shot fired. They remember workers imbibing the local German beers before a begrudging return to work, pubs on every corner, and neighborhood kids playing baseball at Taft Field—a four-field baseball park, lively with children from all around the urban basin.

As John and Karen aged in Camp Washington, they started a social club for friends and music acquaintances from their band days, cleverly named CODA—Cincinnati Oldies Doo-Wop Association. "Coda" is also a musical term for the last refrain of a song. They had regular Friday night musical acts that filled the room, so much so that their members were spilling out of Taft Field Tavern, and they had to find a larger venue on the east side of

Cincinnati. Their club became a victim of its own success, and they started a new social club in Camp called DOT, which stands for Downtown Old Timers. A core group of thirty people swelled to 150, a testament to how beloved they are in their community.

John and Karen remember the decline, but they also remember the vibrancy—a neighborhood of characters—all with stories and struggles and a fondness for their community. For those of us that study cities, like myself, we evaluate urban fabric as a dry diagnostic exercise.

We tell stories in graphs and measure neighborhood vibrancy in terms of the markers of investment and wealth that we've been trained to value. We owe it to ourselves, and these places, to find and tell the stories of neighborhoods agnostic of our metrics. As the gas piping in our ceiling taught us, we're prone to understand at a superficial level unless we are willing to peel back what's only visible at the surface.

East Westwood: Where the Sidewalk Ends

ANNETTE J. WICK

I stand at the intersection where Westwood Northern Boulevard dips into Baltimore Avenue. Te'Airea Powell, a resident of East Westwood, is at my side as we gaze across the street. Beneath telephone pole signs for "Buying all cars / running or not," a scratched concrete square of sidewalk abruptly stops at Baltimore's western edge. The juncture is a major cross street in one of Cincinnati's western neighborhoods called East Westwood. Here, there are occasional views of former woolen mills and workshops in the Mill Creek valley while the University of Cincinnati campus pokes up on the other side of that yawning valley, which divides the west side from the rest of the city. The sidewalk, which should carry on along the northern side of a bustling thoroughfare, would protect any of its 3,000 residents who are on their way to apartments or temple, those whose lives circle this approximate one square mile.

Powell grew up here, moved away, and returned to make it home. At the time, she had been running for Cincinnati City Council, but as of late, she has spent most of her time rushing to meetings following the June shooting of two children, ages six and eight, who were caught in the crossfire at a nearby troubled convenience market.

We have met on a misty morning at the 1930s colonial-style sanctuary of Third Presbyterian Church, or "Third Church," to walk East Westwood. Nothing here is far. Not the market, the church, or the interrupted sidewalk that should connect the rest of the neighborhood—but doesn't.

On January 24, 1990, at the will of residents who desired to separate from neighboring Westwood, the city of Cincinnati stitched together thoroughfares and backstreets and established its fifty-first neighborhood, East Westwood.

In a 1991 *Cincinnati Enquirer* interview, resident and future president of the East Westwood Improvement Association Nancy Broering, said, "We'd been in limbo for years." Later, she commented, "Our initial intentions were not to become a separate entity. We wanted to improve our neighborhood" to break through the isolation many around her felt.

A new name and a carve-out from surrounding neighborhoods, the thinking went, would bring more money and an answer to the area's longtime identity crisis. A fresh influx of residents, where a majority lived in multifamily units and another third resided in single-family homes, would boost their demographics.

Demographic information and maps on the city's website demarcate East Westwood's current boundaries, which are shaped like a frying pan. Its borders touch seven other neighborhoods: Westwood, Mount Airy, Roll Hill, Millvale, English Woods, North and South Fairmont. There's no industry here. But there's a hair salon, a second-generation dental practice, and Roll Hill School, serving preschool through sixth grade, which sits on a back hill of the neighborhood.

Sitting a bit forgotten, and nestled in the hills on the city's near west side, East Westwood is an island whose character has shifted with the prevailing winds of inherited wealth, city attention—or lack thereof—and resident engagement. Once home to Major Daniel Gano, who acted as advisor in the War of 1812 and lived in what is now East Westwood from 1860 to 1873, was the community itself defined by past planning and land plotting, or by the work of members who were now seated beneath the rafters of the Third Presbyterian Church?

The cream-colored, one-story structure is East Westwood's cornerstone, literally and figuratively. Founded in 1835 and subsequently moved from the West End, the church is the one location everyone knows. It's where children gather to play on new basketball courts, partially funded by a partnership with an east-side church. As Rodney Christian, president of the East Westwood Community Council, said about helpful relationships, "Just get us started and let us go for it, because I think that's good for the community."

The basketball courts, with a fence placard that reads, "Walk with the wise and become wise," shine through the spray of rain in their blocks of yellow and maroon paint.

The church's annual report accounts for feeding kids six days a week, friendship and mentoring on their lower level, and maintaining their grounds. Community associations meet regularly and engage with the media, and members run for office. And across the street, a communal garden thrives.

On our walk together, Powell and I move from the church, past a woman tending a rock-lined garden bursting with bird feeders and whirligig flowers. After the June shooting, Powell spoke out against politicians' deriding parents for not watching their children, and she welcomed reporters, who were surprised to see residents watering those flowers.

Our first stop beyond the garden is a crescent-shaped bus pullover for an active route, where residents assemble around a single, low concrete bench. Nearby, a faded yellow and green wood-carved East Westwood sign from its founding days is nearly erased by weeds.

It's difficult to discern where the center of East Westwood is located. There is no square—"like in Oakley or other neighborhoods," as Powell says—so I consider the bus stop the beating heart of this living system until we come upon another focal point: a traffic island designed to slow cars driving along McHenry.

Powell points to a soaring pine tree rising up from the island. She beams when telling me the community lights it up at Christmastime.

"We're working with the parks department for a better electric source and to help us clean up this island. Remove or replace the busted concrete planter. That would never be allowed to sit like that in Hyde Park or downtown."

If community leaders like Powell and others have their way, it won't be allowed here either. East Westwood has joined with other west-siders, including councilpersons, to address the recent round of violence and lack of city commitments. Their voice is strong. It is alive and present.

It's evident what this small patch means to those living nearby and to Powell, who returned to pour her confidence and energy into the community.

The Price Hills: Diaspora from the Bottoms

SARAH THOMAS

My family's history in Cincinnati is rooted in Price Hill. But to understand it, you have to start in the Bottoms.

West Third Street at Central Avenue, now called Queensgate, is a paved intersection with four corners of parking lots just one block from I-75.

On May 1, 1948, its then-cobblestone streets held the weight of 300-plus wedding guests sending off my Lebanese grandparents as they joyously left St. Anthony of Padua Church. They had both grown up in "the Bottoms," living modestly but flourishing in the true American dream—an immigrant community building a new generational home.

Less than a decade later, that home would need to find a new location—centralized in a western haven known as Price Hill, but also scattered across the dense neighborhoods of Cincinnati—as the Bottoms were demolished.

But let's rewind just a bit.

"The Bottoms" spanned Cincinnati's riverfront, giving life to bustling streets and historic tenement buildings that housed a sizable and tight-knit community of Lebanese immigrants. Lila, my "Sitti," was shaped by her life on Third Street, buying five-cent ice creams on the corner before boarding the Island Queen steamboat to Coney Island.

Each passing year was memorialized by the family photographs taken at Rensler's photography on Court and Vine. Her parents worked in the factories to provide a modest home made into a dream childhood by the powerful community around them. As first-generation Americans, Lila and Eddie prepared to build their life, bolstered by a unique love and pride only immigrant families can offer.

By 1955, St. Anthony of Padua Church was torn down, along with the rest of the neighborhood, to make way for futuristic automobile infrastructure and Fort Washington Way. The city and state collaborated under the guise of "urban renewal" to obliterate "the Bottoms," just as they did the nearby West End.

On paper, their federal funding "removed blight" and demolished buildings, while in reality, they uprooted families and erased a flourishing community in the name of ill-thought progress. As I sit, waiting for traffic lights to change, I can't help but imagine all the lives those streets birthed, fostered, and ultimately lost.

Our family moved to small homes on Purcell Avenue in Price Hill, still driving to St. Anthony of Padua every Sunday. The new church on Victory Parkway in East Walnut Hills erupted with Arabic conversation and the familiarity of previous lives lived in other parts of town and other parts of the world.

They began to build another new life in Price Hill: working in the neighborhood, befriending neighbors, and sending their boys to Holy Family School. After becoming a young widow, Sitti found her social support everywhere: neighbors in Price Hill, dinners at St. Anthony, grocery deliveries from Findlay Market vendors.

Here in Cincinnati, we observe a sharp delineation between the multiple Price Hills—East, West, and Lower. But my family's history observes no such boundaries.

Sitti lived six and a half decades in Price Hill, raising her sons on Purcell and Bassett and later raising me on Glenway.

Living just west of the bend where Glenway meets Rapid Run, we grew up in a modest apartment made more special by the familiarity of the neighborhood's special places. As a young child, it felt like Sitti's balcony overlooking the neighboring woods was the top of the world, bolstered by St. Lawrence Bakery pickups, panoramic visits to Mount Echo Park, and warm greetings from neighbors on each porch we passed on our afternoon walks.

As diaspora, our paths spread out far from a single home base. Our traditions spanned the city, grasping at the memories of home in many places.

We spent summers driving to Coney Island long after the Island Queen retired, holidays seeing the CG&E (Duke) holiday trains and Fountain Square trees, and attending gatherings at St. Anthony for the twice-annual "Taste of Lebanon."

We found our home in our afternoon walks down Glenway, weekly grocery stops to Dean's Mediterranean at Findlay Market in Over-the-Rhine, and monthly visits to St. Anthony's Ladies Sodality. My first apartment was in East Walnut Hills, two blocks from St. Anthony's.

Each place held a piece of our community, completing the puzzle of a home. Sitti spent the last year of her life in my home in Northside, eating meals brought home from Findlay Market.

Though the family life spanned the urban core of Cincinnati, when Sitti went to her final home, it was in Price Hill. She is buried in the St. Joseph New Cemetery, which appropriately sits on the border of East and West Price Hill. She lies alongside her beloved husband, Eddie, and parents, Abla and Charles.

Despite the trips to plant flowers on their graves, my young brain never grasped the proximity of their resting place to our home. The gap widens as the years pass and life pulls us further away. It's now my twice-annual trips to flower their graves that bring back the flashes of memory of both person and place.

Price Hill continues to chart its future. The St. Lawrence Bakery is gone, but hope springs eternal along Warsaw as community development births new resources and life. The current intersection of Elberon and Bassett boasts vacant storefronts across from the mini-mart; contrasting the old "Mr. T's Pizza" run by cousins across from one of the apartments that housed Sitti and Eddie in their honeymoon years. Sometimes surprising even myself, the fleeting memories rush back in pristine detail as I recognize less and less of the current neighborhood.

The familiarity of Price Hill, somehow the same and yet completely different, provides ethereal connections to love and loss. Every visit to West Price Hill replays afternoons in Rapid Run Park.

But like my family, the memories don't stay contained within the borders of the Price Hills. Every holiday weekend spent downtown recalls the joy of childhood Christmas displays. Every drive down Victory Parkway summons the memories of St. Anthony festivals in the parking lot.

As neighborhoods change and our own paths veer, our homes ebb and flow. Our communities are built on the backs of our neighbors and the love we share. Some are lucky to hold their home in one place; some find it waiting around each corner of our city. Our communities shape us just as much as we shape them, but the fabric of home is held together by the familiar places in between.

Westwood: More than Cincinnati's Texas

GREG HAND

Overheard in a Western Hills watering hole as a native attempted to guide a visitor through local arcana: "Westwood is like Cincinnati's Texas. It's big. It's out west. It's conservative. And it tried to secede."

While all of that is—kind of—accurate, don't push the Texas comparison in earshot of a Westwoodian. They're likely to push back.

It's true that Westwood is big. It's big enough that it has its own neighborhoods. The historic business district along Harrison Avenue has a very different "feel" from the vast parking lots and big-box stores lining Glenway Avenue. Garden-adorned cul-de-sacs off Glenmore Avenue contrast with apartment complexes piled up along the Montana Avenue hill. Westwood is the largest of Cincinnati's fifty-two neighborhoods both in terms of raw acreage and by population, with around 30,000 residents. Ten percent of all Cincinnatians live in Westwood.

While there really was a recent discussion about secession, it was led by a few vocal cranks and went nowhere. Ironically, Westwood never wanted to be part of Cincinnati and, in fact, voted against annexation in 1896. Westwood is a Cincinnati neighborhood today because George Barnsdale Cox, the infamous turn-of-the-century political fixer known as "Boss" Cox, rewrote the rules and got a state law allowing him to annex Westwood despite the votes of its residents. For the record, Westwood voted against annexation to Cincinnati 149 to 120.

And it is true that, once annexed, Westwood settled into a century of serene conservatism, eschewing the social trends that shaped Cincinnati and resisting efforts to diversify or modernize. In spite of this inertia, Westwood evolved.

From 1990 to 2010, Westwood lost population, declining from 36,496 residents in 1990 to around 30,000 in the 2010 census. In 1980, Westwood was 95 percent white, transitioning to around 48 percent white in 2010. Changes in zoning, economics, and demographics—primarily age and income—led to an influx of multifamily rental units. Although the historic business district remains solidly middle-class, parts of Westwood contain many households below the poverty line.

For a time, Westwood reacted with fear. An organization sounded the alarm with the motto, "It's your neighborhood. Keep it clean. Keep it safe. Take it back." Westwood became known as the neighborhood that said "No!" to everything. Some of the malcontents grumbled about seceding from Cincinnati.

The last straw, for many residents, was a mural. Artworks had successfully commissioned murals all over the city, and some Westwoodians wanted a mural in their community. The nay-saying crowd went apoplectic, warning of dire consequences if paint was applied to a vacant wall at Joe Henke's winery, one of the few viable businesses in a desolately empty business district. Despite resistance from the official civic organizations, a small group of Westwood residents banded together in 2010 to get the mural painted and ceremoniously unveiled.

Emboldened by their success and frustrated at the negative reputation Westwood had earned, the veterans of the mural effort formed Westwood Works, an initiative to promote new and positive energy in the neighborhood. A decade later, the effects are astounding. Muse Café opened in a vacant storefront, and an old sign shop was converted into West Side Brewing.

It's been said that Muse Café is Westwood's living room and West Side Brewing is the neighborhood's lively rathskeller. An unused Bell Telephone switching station now houses the Madcap Education Center, offering training and performances in puppetry, acting, music, dance, and fine arts. An abandoned firehouse was transformed into Nation Kitchen and Bar. A plumbing supply depot is now Wondercade, a modern arcade for gamers of all ages and backgrounds. Ivory House, now recognized as one of Cincinnati's finest restaurants, brings diners from throughout the region to what had been a derelict savings and loan.

Westwood suffered a stinging defeat in 2013 when the historic home of James N. Gamble, son of the cofounder of Procter & Gamble and inventor of Ivory soap, was demolished after months of protest. When the owners of that iconic property announced their intention to sell the estate in 2020, Westwood residents banded together to connect the Great Parks of Hamilton County and the Cardinal Land Trust in a successful effort to create a new county park.

Today, Westwood's calendar is loaded with events to bring people together and to raise funds for neighborhood improvements. The second Saturdays of June, July, August, and September jam the Town Hall District with festivals for thousands of residents and guests. The September Second Saturday coincides with the annual Westwood Art Show. Westwood's

Multicultural Fest, Halloween fundraiser, and Yuletide merriments round out the year.

The work for progress continues. A group of Westwood residents initiated a movement for change in the racially divided community. Adopting the name One Westwood, the organizers have challenged residents to bridge the racial divide by engaging all sectors of the community in conversation and by inspiring action to build equity. One Westwood was recognized by the Urban League with its 2019 Journey Award in celebration of community transformation through inclusion, equity, and partnership.

Challenges remain. An effort to calm traffic through the historic district proceeds by fits and starts. The decrepit business district centered on the Harrison and McHenry intersection needs some love. As real estate prices rise, affordable housing gains importance. But despite the challenges, Westwood is focused now on the positive and the possible.

EAST

Evanston: Hope after the Highway

CARRIE RHODUS

Marye Ward's grandparents weren't permitted to buy a house in Evanston—until a white friend helped them out.

In the 1950s, there was an unofficial barrier on Montgomery Road: Black families stayed to the west, and white families stayed to the east. The Evanston Civic Association tried to block white homeowners from selling to Black families. But in 1954, a Black Episcopal priest purchased a house on Hewitt Avenue.

"So, actually what happened, my grandparents who lived downtown in the West End weren't able to purchase a home in Evanston before it was a predominantly Black community," Ward says. "The story that I got from granddaddy was that they had a white friend that went to bat for them to get the house, and my grandmother being very fair with straight hair, the house was sold to her. So, once we got in, her brother bought a house on Clarion and that's the same house that I live in."

Over the next three years, neighbors resorted to violence and burning crosses in the priest's yard. Many other residents moved out of the neighborhood, leaving Evanston over 80 percent Black.

The village of Evanston was established in 1894. It was named after the Chicago suburb, and founders hoped to create a village that was equally idyllic. Village Council paved the streets, graded the curbs, installed streetlights and concrete sidewalks, and brought in public water and sewer lines. These improvements worked, and the population grew 1,500 percent in less than ten years. The village was annexed into the city of Cincinnati on November 19, 1903, and the neighborhood continued to blossom. It was a prime "streetcar suburb" with easy access to jobs downtown, clean air, and spacious lots. The neighborhood primarily consisted of white, German immigrant families who were equally Protestant and Catholic.

By the 1940s, Evanston was at its peak. There were no vacant lots or abandoned buildings, businesses lined Montgomery Road from end to end, and St. Mark had a congregation of 1,200 families.

However, the end of World War II saw a dramatic change in how Americans were living, working, and commuting. This led to the passage of the Federal Aid Highway Act.

In Cincinnati, the first highway was I-75, which ran directly through the West End neighborhood. The construction displaced thousands of residents, most of whom were Black. As these residents searched desperately for new homes, some moved to first-ring east-side neighborhoods including Avondale, Walnut Hills, and Evanston.

However, the neighborhood remained predominately middle class. Residences were owner occupied and well cared for, not a speck of trash could be seen throughout the neighborhood, and the residents were proud of their neighborhood. Beverley Lamb shared stories from life during this period.

"The business district was actually thriving," Lamb told me. "On Saturdays, I would go around with (my father) and we'd always stop at the barbershop. I don't recall at all the name of the shop, but I learned at an early age that men gossip, because sitting in that barbershop was a hoot. But it's like, if you wanted to know what was going on, uh, you know, just go into the barbershop."

Resident James Stallworth remembers much the same scenes.

"I remember when you could stand at White Castle and look all the way up to Duck Creek and I bet you couldn't find two pieces of paper on the street," he said. "It was just the way peoples took care of their properties back then."

"This area had gaslights and trees down every block," Ward concurs. "It looked like Hyde Park looks now. That's how Evanston looked before the expressway."

Unfortunately, the United States government had other plans. In the 1970s, I-71 was constructed, and the project cut straight through Evanston. The highway destroyed several blocks of residential housing and cut off the northern business district. This led to decades of decline as families were cut off from their community, residents were forced to find a new home for a second time, and businesses were demolished.

"Oh, that changed everything because it broke the business district," Lamb says. "The houses and the people who lived there were displaced. I don't remember anyone in favor of that, but I do remember it created a major upheaval in the community and neighbors were just furious about it because they were never asked. The residents feel that it also split them in half. That you have an upper and a lower Evanston. That's why there's half of Evanston kids who don't use the rec center because they don't feel like they belong there, but it's not that anyone has done anything to them at the rec center—more as if growing up you're in the lower part and not the upper."

Marye Ward agrees.

"Oh, I definitely remember because of how it cut the streets off," she said. "Since my family lived within blocks you could come out the back door and run down the street, turn the corner and you're at my Aunt Johanna's house, cross the street and I'm at my grandparents' house. So, with them cutting off the streets, I lost friends because right there where the highway is, there was an apartment building where kids lived so they're just scattered. Then it just kind of sliced our neighborhood in half."

Fortunately, that isn't true today. The Evanston Community Council is made up of passionate individuals like Lamb, Ward, and Stallworth. They're working to breathe life back into their neighborhood. Successful businesses are starting to pop up and homes are being renovated. There will always be a gnawing hole in the shape of a highway, but they are bridging connections to reunite the community.

Hyde Park East: Funky for a Hundred Years

DANN WOELLERT

When I first moved to Hyde Park East in 1999, I was attracted to its funkiness and proximity to downtown.

It's a place distinct from Hyde Park proper, one of Cincinnati's most prestigious neighborhoods. It's the downstairs to Hyde Park's upstairs. Maybe that's because it was a later annex to Hyde Park, with significantly smaller working-class homes compared to the monstrous Gilded Age mansions of Hyde Park proper.

Hyde Park East offers a compact, walkable residential and business district. Its closeness to cultural and recreational assets are a big plus.

But it's the food scene here that really sets the neighborhood apart, along with the sense of early twentieth-century history remarkably preserved from the neighborhood's early development.

I have always loved the craftsman details of my 1923 home and the walkability to Ault Park at the end of my street. At the time I moved here, there were still bungalows to be had for bargains from some of the original owners or their families. I bought mine from a retired unmarried teacher, the daughter of the man who built it. I spent the next several years renovating while preserving its original craftsman character.

Others have taken wilder rehab paths. Take the Mushroom House, the work of UC professor of architecture Terry Brown. He transformed his one-bedroom bungalow into an eclectic piece of public art and his studio between 1992 and 2006. It never would have flown in Hyde Park proper, where they complain about house paint colors along Erie Avenue.

I have also enjoyed being able to walk to Coffee Emporium, one of the anchors of the neighborhood. Husband-and-wife team Tony Tausch and Eileen Schwab, former employers of locally based consumer goods giant Procter & Gamble, started on Hyde Park Square in 1973. They moved to their current Hyde Park East location in 1978. Then they expanded to a second shop in Over-the-Rhine in 2002. They have a nice backyard garden—perfect for eating pancakes on a late Sunday morning. I'm a huge fan of their spitzbuben cookie—or jam-filled thumbprint.

Though it is distinct in identity and personality, you have to understand the history of Hyde Park proper to understand HPE. The former had been established as a village in 1896 and annexed to Cincinnati in 1903. The name both neighborhoods share comes from Hyde Park, New York, named after Edward Hyde, Lord Cornbury, the colonial governor of the state from 1702 to 1708. Lord Cornbury was a distinctive character—he made big news in 1702 when he opened the New York Assembly in drag, wearing, in the fashion of England's Queen Anne, a hooped gown and elaborate headdress and sporting a fan.

The land where HPE sits now was annexed to Cincinnati in 1909, the same year the Hyde Park Country Club on Erie Avenue opened.

A man named William Harmon developed Hyde Park East in the 1910s. Before the houses came, Harmon added fourteen brick masonry columns along each intersection on Erie Avenue, topped with planters, to promote the new area. There are only five still standing, one of which stands at the entrance to my subdivision. It's topped with a winged gargoyle, our own version of the *Manneken Pis* statue in Belgium. He's been dressed in a Santa hat, bunny ears, leprechaun hat, and even as an *alebrijas* for Dia de los Muertos.

Harmon moved on to Chicago, where he developed more neighborhoods. When he died in 1926, it was revealed that he used the nickname Jedediah Tingle, the mysterious philanthropist who made generous financial gifts to great writers, obscure poets, unsung heroes, and good children without ever revealing his true identity.

The #69 streetcar along Erie Avenue helped promote growth of HPE during the 1920s, including occupancy of the large Ravenswood apartment building on Erie by about 1930. The small one-bedroom cottages on Tarpis behind the police station were built to house the mostly single streetcar operators. By 1939, some of the small shops had changed their names from family names to Hyde Park East Dry Cleaning or Hyde Park East Shoe Repair, indicating a rise in HPE's identity as its own neighborhood.

These days, Hyde Park has about 1,200 units of housing, mostly two- or three-bedroom craftsman-era cottages like mine. More than 60 percent are occupied by their owners, contrasted with Cincinnati's 40 percent owner-occupancy rate. Home values, while still high compared to Cincinnati's median prices overall, are about a third of the median prices of Hyde Park homes. Hyde Parkers are always quick to point out the "East" when an "Easter" leaves it off the description.

The architecture is cool. Even cooler? Something about the neighborhood—perhaps its proximity to sophisticated Hyde Park, but with slightly lower real estate prices—has made it a hotbed for food innovation.

Where to start with that? Maybe at the home of the Helen Goelitz family, which sat on the border of Hyde Park and HPE at the corner of Delta and Griest, next to St. John Park.

Helen's sons Adolph and Herman Goelitz introduced America to candy corn, a candy made from a new butter cream manufacturing technology. Their sister Joanna married Edward Kelley in Cincinnati in 1902, and their son would run what would become the Jelly Belly Corporation in California, which is still making candy corn according to the same recipe that was introduced in Cincinnati.

And then there are the restaurants—the creations of unique individuals who were ahead of their time here in Cincinnati, or who at least knew how to start something that lasts.

Long before the downtown restaurant bubble, a two-block section of Erie became a playground for hyperfusion international cuisine in Cincinnati. The first block to take on this fusion cuisine is a series of connected 1920s-era one-story neighborhood shops at Erie and Amberson.

One of the first Thai restaurants on the east side, Bangkok Bistro took over a vacated Snappy Tomato Pizza joint in the complex in 1994 and introduced Pad Thai and Choo Chee to many East-siders. They paved the way for Lemongrass on Madison, Ruthai's on Linwood, and Wild Ginger on Edwards.

Then, in the early 2000s, Chef "Yaj" Udyaya and Tunisian native Alex Mchaikl, renovated a former taco restaurant in that same complex, creating a very small boutique Indian restaurant called Cumin. Cumin expanded into a larger spot next door, then it became Ash in 2013, and now Café Mediterranean, owned by Fahri Ozdil. The small original Cumin space became an Israeli restaurant, then M, a wood-fired pizza place, and now it's Forno Osterio + Bar. Forno has a wild boar with chocolate sauce—*cinghiale in cocciolato*—that's as authentic as the same dish I had in Montelpuciano, Italy, at the Café Polizano.

Around the corner at Saybrook and Erie is another late 1920s cluster of shops that has housed great restaurants since the 1930s.

The history of one of these storefronts in particular shows you the progression of East Hyde Park's dining scene.

The end shop at 2672 Erie first housed the Saybrook Tavern, a family restaurant specializing in steaks and seafood that was known for their kissing fish mural in the dining room. The owner, James Morgenroth, operated a butcher shop next door and then opened the Saybrook Tavern in 1946.

He served as president of the local arm of the National Restaurant Association and would operate the tavern until 1976. Morgenroth sold to his manager, David Walsh, who then sold it to the next owner in 1984, when it became Pasta al Dente. PAD was fantastic and always packed—they dished huge portions at great prices. Serving homemade ravioli and cannelloni and stuffed zucchini, it was great for us recent, poor college graduates who could make three meals out of a trip.

In 2005, owner Jay Scavo decided to close Pasta al Dente. The space was then taken over by Merritt Oleksi, a culinarian from Boston, and Charlie Choi, a local Asian restauranteur, and named Sake Bomb. The two pioneered sushi in suburban Cincinnati. Choi would go on to open Dancing Wasabi on Edwards, in the old Beluga restaurant space, and then Mr. Sushi downtown.

In 2011, 2672 Erie would become Saigon Café, a Vietnamese and sushi restaurant, under Alex Ng. I spent many a "half-price sushi" night there eating a Hyde Park roll made of spicy tuna, cucumber, avocado, and tempura flakes. Saigon closed in 2016, and the space has held a succession of eateries since.

That's the charm of Hyde Park East in a nutshell. The sense of continuity going back a century mixed with the dynamic changes make it a place that is exciting and comforting all at once. Less fancy than her older sister, HPE looks great at 100 and is always willing to try new things.

Mount Lookout:
The Lights of My Neighbors
ROB PASQUINUCCI

The flyer arrived along with the first pile of mail at the new house—a note promoting the Mount Lookout Luminaria event coming that weekend. Our Christmas tree was hastily displayed in the corner of the living room, and decorations were still being unpacked, but seeing the streets of our neighborhood lined with candles in white paper bags that night was special, and it was the first of many moments we'd have where we found ourselves falling in love with our neighborhood.

While it's a few miles from the city's core, Mount Lookout has been a part of Cincinnati since the late 1800s. At the time, the area was countryside, where Catawba grapes used to make wine grew.

Much of today's neighborhood was part of the Kilgour estate. The Kilgour brothers were part of the Mornington Syndicate, the group who developed Mount Lookout, Oakey, and Hyde Park. Around this time, the Cincinnati Observatory moved to its current location in the neighborhood, allowing generations to look at the night sky on starry nights. A branch railroad line linked the neighborhood to more developed parts of Cincinnati in 1872. That line terminated where Mount Lookout Square is today.

As a history nerd, I love living in a place with a past that lives on in the present—from stately homes on tree-lined streets, to buildings that line the square and, of course, the observatory.

Our house has a phone niche—one of those little built-in shelves where the phone would sit. I found a period-correct phone to put in there. I like to imagine families that lived here before us gathering around that phone to reach out to loved ones on holidays before phones were something we all have in our pocket. One of Bell System's original central office buildings is a large and beautiful colonial-style structure on Delta Avenue. I believe at one time it housed the many mechanical switches that were required to place a call in a more analog world.

I dug up archive photos of our street from the University of Cincinnati archives and found not much has changed in seventy years. The light poles look different, and SUVs have replaced chromed behemoths with tailfins, but the homes are the same.

Before moving here, we already had memories of Mount Lookout. My wife and I had our first date at Ruthai's Thai restaurant, we took our wedding photos at Ault Park, and a friend who lives in the neighborhood held some amazing parties at his home. In the summer, we'd make our way to the concert series at Ault Park and were already fans of the Fourth of July fireworks celebration. But moving here did more than put us within walking distance to things we already loved. It gave us a chance to meet and make friends with the great people who live here.

Among the first neighbors we met was a guy known as the mayor of our street. I'm not sure how he got that title, but he served us well—often throwing impromptu Friday evening happy hours in his driveway, taking the lead in organizing annual block parties and potlucks, and always offering a friendly hello and conversation to his constituents when out and about. When he was battling cancer, he'd force his failing body to join in street parties. When cancer took him, it was the Mount Lookout version of a state funeral. He is remembered with a tree planted in his memory in Ault Park.

As we walked our kids around the neighborhood, we met more great people, all willing to lend a hand, whether it's helping to lift a heavy package, shoveling a sidewalk, or keeping an eye on a kid or dog for a minute. Each day, we get a chance to catch up as we walk kids to and from school—learning who's moving in, who's moving out, and who is having what done to their house.

Now, when the Fourth of July comes around each year, we invite many of these friends and neighbors over to catch the fireworks on our front lawn. We have a great view, at least until the trees a few streets over get too tall.

I've had the chance to support the neighborhood by serving as president of the Mount Lookout Community Council. I'm proud to continue this group's tradition by working with city leaders to plan for the area's future and by holding annual events, including a Fall Fest on Mount Lookout Square and the popular Luminaria event. We had big plans to celebrate the neighborhood's 150th year in 2020, however the COVID-19 outbreak limited what we could do.

It's totally cliché, but I'll say it anyway—the neighborhood's greatness isn't just the quaint tree-lined streets, historic homes, and proximity to parks—it's the people who have chosen to build their lives here, working together.

Madisonville: The Double Bind

ERIC EBLE

The intersection of Madison and Plainville confounds drivers.

The three-way stop forces north- and southbound traffic to wait for motorists headed east on Madison to turn left toward Madeira or (more rarely) to speed straight into E. Fork Avenue. Cars have the option of heading southward to Mariemont prior to reaching that intersection with a gradual curve, which does not include a stop. Those waiting at stop signs give complete deference to people entering the area; one can tell that an uninitiated outsider has arrived by an SUV (it's usually an SUV) stopping at the three-way intersection and waving the cars, awaiting their turn to go ahead, leading to the exchange of single- and multifingered gestures.

In terms of metaphors for neighborhoods, this one is perfect for examining my home of seven years, Madisonville—though, as a former head of a neighborhood improvement nonprofit dedicated to installing gardens in my area of Cincinnati reminded me, "You *actually* live in Madison Place." Tough words coming from a resident of Sycamore Township, but . . . sure. Madison Place it is, Mr. Green Carpetbagger.

One might point to another iconic symbol of the neighborhood—the Madisonville train bridges—as the best source of metaphor to describe this offshoot of Cincinnati (which, when examined on a by-neighborhood map, resembles a heat-warped and bloated version of Alaska), which was incorporated into the Queen City in 1911 and named after America's fourth president.

The black-backed bridges don't read "Welcome to Madisonville!" or "Madisonville: The Friendly Place"; instead, the white font simply shouts, "MADISONVILLE," demarcating a line in the sand that one has just crossed instead of waving a welcome. "Hey, you are here," it says. "Take it or leave it." The metaphor grows in hilarity when one considers that traffic halts around the bridge when some unthinking truck driver tries to pass under said bridge, only to be stuck until a tow truck can pull him out—an occurrence that causes plenty of laughter for my seven-year-old daughter who enjoys *America's Funniest Videos* and my almost-four-year-old son who loves trucks and practical jokes.

But, no, the image of commercial traffic stopped due to oversight does not best capture the spirit of my adopted neighborhood, for several such enterprises have entered this area in the scope of habitation in this "up-and-coming" residential district. *Cincinnati* magazine included Madisonville in its "Next Hot Neighborhoods" list in 2015, claiming it,

> May be something of an underdog in the Cincinnati Neighborhood Olympics. . . . The area began to decline in the 1960s, and signs of that are plentiful. But there is magic in the district's moody atmospherics—its railway trestles and Italian Villa houses, some of which are landmarked in the Madison-Stewart Historic District. The area draws creative types who like the affordable rents, sleepy pace, and the integrity of so much of the vintage architecture, including a number of old churches.

Though I wasn't around for the "decline," a local sage—a former teacher and current poet and gardener, nestled in the Erie Avenue corner of Madisonville—instructs on the dynamics of it.

"You should have seen this place in the 'crack eighties,'" he told me once while my daughter and I surveyed his plants and chicken yard. "Shootings happened there, there, and there." He pointed at various places adjacent to his garden, which he shares with a neighbor who agreed to let him grow on his plot. "This place was dangerous."

Despite that danger, he and his wife—a potter who owned the since-defunct Madison Clayworks—raised their two sons there. "Creative types," I suppose, have long been drawn to Madisonville. I guess we fit that mold; my partner—a classically trained French horn player and elementary music teacher transitioning into a fix-all handywoman—and me—a quasi-hipster high school English teacher who tries to write poetry on the side—qualify, though the rents and pace have increased in the time we have lived here.

In an area with some urban blight and a ton of authentic charm, as well as an 82 percent increase in median home price since 2010, one doesn't have to read the tea leaves to see gentrification at work—the people at the three-way stop have to sit idly by as people enter their neighborhood recklessly. On paper, these businesses speak to people like my partner and me: We have dogs, we like Oaxacan tacos, and we want to be fit. Taking into account the coffee shops and the more recent additions of upscale housing developments at the corner of Madison and Whetsel, one would assume that this "sleepy" hood has admitted enough traffic to move away from its underdog status. If the Tap and Screw microbrewery had remained open, we coulda been a contender.

Alas, *Cincinnati* magazine *did* bump Madisonville upward in the standings of its neighborhoods; a 2019 article entitled "The Best-Bang-For-Your-Buck Neighborhoods in Cincinnati" proclaims, "If you're one of the lucky folks already living in Madisonville, stay put. Why? It's one of Cincinnati's hottest neighborhoods for existing home sales right now. It's also close to the city's urban core and chock-full of well-maintained historic properties. Word on the street is redevelopment is finally coming, too."

I suppose I shouldn't be too hard on *Cincinnati* magazine; Madisonville deserves excitement. My family lucked into a house that's wedged between a kind seventy-something who feeds every cat in the neighborhood and a since-deceased lifer who raised her four children in the Cape Cod next door, forcing them to get along together in the one shared upstairs bedroom. We can walk with our children and other neighborhood kids to the Good Shepherd Montessori playground, deemed a "naturescape," and, along the way, greet a population diverse in age, race, and socioeconomic standing. We have a dive bar, the Bramble Patch (referred to by some as "the Bramble" and others as "the Patch"), that (prior to COVID-19) hosted Bengals potlucks and served the waitstaff of various Mariemont restaurants. To boot, we can walk to those restaurants without having to suffer the higher cost of living.

But the preference to outside development—the cars entering Madisonville at the three-way stop—proves maddening, as the neighborhood faces the double bind of gentrification: better amenities at the cost of those in the neighborhood who may not have access to them. Take, for example, a simple fact that dawned on me recently: Madisonville is a food desert. The USDA definition fits the area—"low-income tracts in which a substantial number or proportion of the population has low access to supermarkets or large grocery stores"—and a zip code search on the USDA's "Food Desert Locator" shows a swath of land, entirely encompassed in Madisonville, that qualifies as such. Adding insult to injury, the neighborhood lost its IGA when it was transformed into a luxury car dealership, trading bread and milk for Porsche and Maserati. A more recent iteration of that transformation occurred when the same dealership acquired a parcel of land including the local Dollar General—the only place even resembling a grocery store—and flattened it for a larger lot.

My narration of this history of encroachment certainly smacks of class consciousness and fist-shaking at the wealthy; "Get off my lawn!" sounds like my battle cry. But this dynamic extends the intersection metaphor for

Madisonville even further, considering the new, sleek foreign makes and models moving through my neighborhood from well-to-do suburbs like Mariemont, Indian Hill, and Madeira in contrast to the kaleidoscope of clunkers and antiques moving within Madisonville.

I suppose, though, that anger comes from a tangible concern about the neighborhood's integrity, as well as its safety. My house sits on the end of another odd intersection, a hard-right turn to Mariemont at the top of a hill, on a thru street without stop signs all the way to Plainville; thus, those Mercedes and BMWs speeding down my street threaten my children crossing it to visit their friends. Recently, a sinkhole opened on the road in front of our new neighbor's house, and city workers placed a cone in its center for a week to warn drivers, many of whom slowed down to go around it. Yet, a number of drivers simply ran it over or exited their cars to throw the cone into someone's yard. My antipathy about these people fits the damn-the-man narrative in the neighborhood against drive-thru wealth; another longtime resident down the road (our "chicken mama" who supplied our first round of fowl for our backyard coop) told us that her attempts to insert a stop sign at an intersection by her house resulted in higher-ups basically telling her that a kid would have to be run over for such a change to occur.

I clearly cannot cry gentrification innocently; Madisonville isn't OTR, development could eventually bring a grocery store, and I certainly fit the mold of the hipster colonizer. But I also cannot stomach the drive-by ignorance inflicted upon such a wonderful and diverse neighborhood. Beyond its capacity to enhance road rage, the Madison-Plainville intersection has likely caused many accidents as people of varying automotive quality and socioeconomic status try to navigate its wonky traffic rules. Recently, a stop sign popped up at Plainville and Roe, through which a number of cars have sped without stopping, prompting an innate, "Hey, people live here!" shout from behind the wheel of my Prius. Even a stop sign won't stop it, apparently.

And this fraught, lively corridor only stands to increase its confusion and traffic woes. About a half-mile south, a rival to the Madison-Plainville three-way stop is emerging in the five-way Murray-Plainville-Madisonville Road intersection, with a byzantine one-way/left-turn-only system that also confuses many drivers. And there will soon be another variable: an extension of the Murray Road bike path as part of the Wasson Way trail. On a recent run toward the newly constructed start of this trail, I narrowly avoided collision with a Yukon full of blue-shirted children and a mom raging at me from behind the wheel, driving straight in a left-turn-only lane, yelling at me to "Get off the road" as she also almost crashed into a conversion van. As I shook my head, I ran across the road to the trail, where a biker yelled at me to "get on my side" as he swerved to avoid me.

East Walnut Hills: The Parade

KATHY Y. WILSON

It started throughout Walnut Hills the same way it always has in the Black, "depressed" enclaves of neighborhoods across America.

It started with a parade.

Yoga-panted-latte-sipping-dog-walking-noses-in-the-latest-iPhone white folks.

Mostly young.

When I say "depressed," I mean corners and spots that aren't aesthetically pretty—food deserts blotted with bodegas and check-cashing joints, absent of flowerpots, quaint street lighting, and marked pedestrian crosswalks.

According to ZipDataMaps.com—the first Google offering after a "borders of Walnut Hills" search—Walnut Hills is populated by 1,633 people, 80.6 percent of whom are Black. There is a 4.4 percent unemployment rate.

Walnut Hills is bordered by wealthy white neighborhoods on some of its boundaries and by historically Black and lower-income neighborhoods on others.

It's this schizophrenic proximity to white wealth, Black poverty, Black working-class and mixed-race urban Appalachia that I think has long given Walnut Hills some kind of geographic identity crisis.

For the thirty-two years I've been living here—all within a one-mile radius of myself throughout four dwellings—I have witnessed firsthand the neighborhood's struggle with what it's wanted to be.

Instead of marching bands, cheerleaders, drill teams, and mini-car-driving, Fez-wearing Kiwanis, parades in soon-to-be whitewashed Black neighborhoods are inundated with unceasing processions of exotic dogs.

Dog breeds rife in the ghetto—whatever "ghetto" means to you—are menacing guards: pit bulls, Doberman pinschers, rottweilers. Cross the street to get way from these dogs. Or, if they prowl your street, call the kids inside when spotted.

Dog breeds of parade marchers are exotic poodle blends, Weimaraners, dalmatians, any manner of rambunctious border collies and Labradors.

These are dogs that wear clothes, dressed up for the parade.

Suddenly, along these new/old parade routes are new creature comforts, things the indigenous Negro (me) apparently did not heretofore need, desire, or know she needed.

Things like coffeeshops with laboriously prepared cups of coffee and sandwiches packed with precious ingredients; art galleries; themed bars that change with the drinking whims of the drunken, disrespectful patrons who come with them; organic pet food stores and the illegally parking, disrespectful patrons who come with them; bars, bars, and bars.

The nouveau riche pilgrims venturing into my neighborhood render me a foreigner. We longtime Black residents are outcasts. Many of us are priced out in our own land.

And the old neighborhood is now a movie set, idyllic and marketable enough for Instagram accounts with photos posted of the architecture, of "things to do" but never of the folks who *live, work, and strive* here.

Meanwhile, bus routes instituted to serve the convenience of we strivers get sporadic or rerouted, or they disappear altogether. The working people living here for two, sometimes three generations now walk farther to wait longer to pay more fare for our sole transportation. All in the name of progress and gentrification.

When the *first* themed bar opened across the street in what used to be the bodega where I copped my Flavor-Ice treats and Bar-B-Q Grippo's, and where I made change for the bus, I constantly leaned out my fire escape window to yell at the drunk white people littering or puking in the street in front of my apartment. At 3:00 a.m., long past last call, they'd hang outside, loudly yelling at a Lyft driver or making drunken next-day brunch plans.

One morning, I'd had enough.

I raised my window, leaned out from my waist.

"Hey!" I yelled. "Can you guys take that somewhere else and move along?"

"You don't like it, you should move," a young white man yelled at me.

"No," I shot back. "*You* should fucking move."

I made a show of letting the group see me dial 911 to lodge a noise complaint. Can't recall if that did any good; however, through the years and iterations of that specific bar, I have lodged so many noise complaints the 911 operator one morning asked: "Is this Miss Wilson?"

I was proud to say, "It is."

Here's a flash: Neighborhoods are neither IG hashtags nor parade routes. Some of us OGs living within these "trending" blocks are not homeowners. However, because we don't own doesn't negate our stakeholder status.

I am a contributor. I made a life here. In doing so, I have helped make *here* what it is.

Since June 2002, when I moved into this apartment, I have gone to Cuba and published a story about it, published a book, traveled to Amsterdam and, again, published a travelogue, toured a play based on my book, and seen it twice produced by the Ensemble Theatre of Cincinnati.

I've grieved the Mother's Day death of my mother here in 2005 and nearly lost my mind in that abyss, fulfilled a dream of teaching at the University of Cincinnati despite having never graduated college, became the Cincinnati and Hamilton County Public Library's first-ever writer in residence, received the Sachs Fund Prize from ArtsWave, and was inducted into the UC Journalism Hall of Fame, respectively.

I witnessed and celebrated two elections of the nation's first Black-identified, biracial president. I killed, then rebirthed my column "Your Negro Tour Guide" in the city's alternative weekly publication.

I became the FlyGirl in the Buttermilk within these walls. I became a brand.

I was diagnosed with congestive heart failure and end-stage renal failure in this apartment. And on this corner, I underwent three forms of dialysis and received a healthy kidney and am now a kidney transplant survivor.

I met and fell in love with my partner, Kandice, while living in this apartment, and together, we alternately relish and bitch about our neighborhood—a lot more so since the COVID-19 pandemic and subsequent quarantine.

This is not the recitation of a resume; rather, it is an example of a real life lived in a real neighborhood fraught with real problems that is neither a white person's fantasy fulfilled, nor a movie set perfect for IG posts.

The life I've made here transcends the streets, the now-upscale apartments, the rowdy bars, the pop-up drug dealers (yes, they are here) serving bar patrons (yes, they do drugs), the sloppy street vomiters, and the loudmouthed Uber fool.

I am *more* than Walnut Hills; yet I *am* Walnut Hills.

I originally chose this neighborhood because of all the bus routes that whizzed through, the proximity to downtown, I-71, Clifton, the bookstore in Hyde Park, the used-to-be grocery store within walking distance and, well, because it was so pleasingly, soulfully, and loudly *Black*.

Blackness did not then and does not now frighten me.

There used to be so many Black kids running these streets I never had a problem shelling out fives to get my driveway shoveled or passing out popsicles on the stoop in the summer. Back then, though, there were sex workers getting off in the shadows of my darkened driveway, errant folks sitting in front of my door when I'd come out, and car handle pullers looking for unlocked doors.

Then neighborhood elementary schools were closed and combined elsewhere. The changes are driving away, yes, the early rough parts. They also ran off many who simply could no longer afford their rents or were kicked out by landlords who stopped offering Section Eight assistance when property values skyrocketed, and they realized the gold mines they'd been sitting on.

I am my neighborhood with all its contradictions and missteps. If I were that miserable, I would simply move, so my life here is far from untenable.

Though I've yet to be priced out by exorbitant rents (in fact, my landlords are wholly reasonable people), I am still rendered invisible by my age, race, gender, poverty, and my lack of ownership. These are all things stalking me in life *outside* this apartment and this neighborhood, so I am used to it.

So.

Just *move* as an answer to the problems other folks have brought here?

Hell naw.

I am invested.

I am here to sit through the parades.

Mount Washington: Front Yard City, Backyard Suburb

MICHAEL HENSON

Mount Washington, the city of Cincinnati's easternmost neighborhood, is nothing like the New Hampshire version. Once you drive to the top of Beechmont Avenue, you won't find yourself on a majestic, snow-covered granite peak looking out over a forested wilderness; instead, you'll be in a small business district surrounded by midsized homes and rental units. The Mount Washington Water Tower is visible for miles, but our humble mount cannot properly be called a mountain at all.

On the map, we look like a polyp extruded from the city and nearly surrounded by Anderson Township, our suburban, next-door neighbor. On garbage day, fifty yards from my house, an Anderson sanitation truck comes from over a mile away to pick up the three cans set out from the houses (mansions, really) that stand a half-mile down a forested private lane. All of those woods (and all of that taxable land) are in Anderson. Front yard city, backyard suburb.

Like most of southwest Ohio, "Mount" Washington is mostly flat, cut through here and there by creek beds and separated from the rest of Cincinnati by the Little Miami River. But the distinctly un-mountainous neighborhood is a mostly pleasant place, and it does have, as compensation for its un-mountainous character, the hilly, wooded, 125-acre Stanbery Park, where, on the Saturday after Halloween, you can bring your slightly used jack-o'-lantern to be flung downhill by a trebuchet at the annual Pumpkin Chuck.

Early leaders laid out Mount Washington as an independent town in 1846. As transportation technology improved, its population and business base grew to the point where the city annexed it in 1911. It was the second-to-last local village the city swallowed up before Kennedy Heights in 1914. The city nibbled away with further small annexations around Mount Washington into the 1960s, but the community was far enough removed geographically to maintain its original small-town character.

Unlike Anderson, Mount Washington is walkable, compact, and diverse. The housing stock runs from multiunit rental projects to mansions. There are a lot of single-family houses on half-acre lots, so much of the housing stock is still within financial reach of working-class, middle-class families. There is a growing population of African Americans. Many of the Appalachian people pressed out of the gentrified sections of the East End found new homes here.

We have everything a true Cincinnati neighborhood needs, starting with a Kroger and a chili parlor. Pizza? We have two: a sit-down (Ramundo's) and a carryout/delivery (LaRosa's). A library? We have that too. A coffeeshop? We have one, but you have to work for it, since it's all the way down at the foot of the "mountain." Schools? We have two great Cincinnati Public K–8 schools, plus a pair of Catholic schools that go through all twelve grades. Plenty of churches. Not too many bars, but we have a medical clinic and a tattoo parlor. You can mail a letter or train in karate or do your laundry or fix a watch or get a haircut or get your taxes done without leaving the neighborhood. And when you're done with it all, you can get buried in the Mount Washington Cemetery.

Problems? We have all the American classics: racial polarization, sexism, and income inequality are all right here, front and center.

But one of the strengths of the neighborhood is that we like to solve problems. People who just want to whine have at least two online forums for that. But for the people willing to take action, we have an active community council and an organization dedicated to combating the opioid epidemic. A group of volunteers maintain a network of food pantries for the hungry. And when the parks had an influx of homeless individuals, residents worked with agencies to help them get into housing.

Almost heaven? Not exactly. But it'll do until you're planted in the Mount Washington Cemetery.

Camp Dennison:
A Hidden Gem Fading

DANI MCCLAIN

There's a phrase I learned a decade ago when a beloved family member had cancer and the prognosis didn't look good: "anticipatory grief." The words describe something like the opposite of longing, a pervasive sense of dread that can make you miss a person even before they're gone.

For years now, I've been grieving in advance for the neighborhood where I was raised and where I live now: Camp Dennison, Ohio. Located seventeen miles northeast of Cincinnati, Camp Dennison is surrounded by Indian Hill to the west, Old Milford and Terrace Park to the south, and Miamiville to the north, with Loveland beyond it. The Little Miami River borders us to the east. State Route 126 is the main drag through our town, which is home to just over 300 people living in 150 households. The house where I live—a ranch built in 1937 by my maternal grandfather's maternal grandparents—sits on that stretch of road, which is alternately known as Glendale-Milford Road. (That the road shares a name with the one that runs through Evendale is a cruel trick meant to confuse anyone trying to reach our neck of the woods for the first time.)

My mom and I moved to that ranch-style home soon after her father suddenly died there in the early 1980s. I was three, and the house with its painted white clapboard and green shutters was my wonderland. My mom's seven sisters and their kids and husbands were always coming and going, as were members of our extended family who were just a short walk away. When my great-great-grandparents moved here from Milford in the 1930s, it was to be closer to their family, and by the time I came along, it still felt like kinfolk were everywhere. Weekends brought card parties, where people cussed and drank their way through games of bid whist. Summertime meant neighborhood kids playing Marco Polo in the in-ground pool my grandparents had put in the backyard, funded in part by profit from their paper route side hustle. The Gap Band or Earth, Wind & Fire provided a soundtrack while ping-pong balls whizzed across the table that was set up outside during warm months and in the living room once temperatures dropped.

Camp Dennison was the center of my world from the time I was a toddler until I left home for college. But for a long time, I was met with blank stares when I told other Cincinnatians where I was from. My answer to that tired question we ask each other, "Where'd you go to high school?" didn't make sense unless you understood how I came to be in the posh Indian Hill School District, and how my mom and her sisters had before me. I didn't live in a mansion on Shawnee Run or in a cookie-cutter two-story in a Kenwood cul-de-sac. No, I was from the part of the district that gave its schools most of their Black kids. I was from the neighborhood that gave the district many of their poor and working-class white kids, too. In those years of the Reagan and Clinton administrations, the race and class dynamics of Camp Dennison flipped simple mainstream narratives on their heads. We were home to Black families with money and white families without.

On the rare occasion that I met a Cincinnatian who *had* heard of Camp Dennison, they would mention the Schoolhouse Restaurant, an eatery up the street that serves fried chicken and mashed potatoes on lazy Susans. My family members attended classes in that white brick building in the years before Indian Hill set up a public education system. If those who had heard of my community didn't know the restaurant, they knew of the Waldschmidt House, built in 1804 by a settler and Revolutionary War veteran from Pennsylvania named Christian Waldschmidt. He built the first paper mill west of Philadelphia around the same time. In 1861, the Union army chose New Germany (the name Waldschmidt had given his settlement) as the site of a military camp where tens of thousands of troops would go on to train and convalesce until it shut down in 1865. The Civil War-era name stuck, and occasionally, I'd meet a history buff who had come across mention of Camp Dennison while researching Harriet Beecher Stowe, the author and abolitionist who lived in Cincinnati for a while, or the Indian Hill cellars rumored to have served as way stations on the Underground Railroad.

It was a pleasant surprise when I met a Cincinnatian who knew of Camp Dennison, but their references usually felt disconnected from the place I knew and loved. To me, the Schoolhouse Restaurant's draw has never been the food but the goats who laze around the pen out back. Petting horses at Derbyshire Stables (near the intersection of Camp and Kugler Mill Roads) and feeding goats at the Schoolhouse are part of the quintessential Camp Dennison childhood. But focusing on either place, like focusing on the early nineteenth-century homestead of a Pennsylvania Dutch settler, obscures what is to me the most interesting part of the community's history: the Black part.

Because of my family's long history here, many novels written by Toni Morrison, a fellow native Ohioan, felt familiar upon first read. *Sula, Paradise*, and *Song of Solomon* in particular contain snatches of stories I feel I've heard before, spoken in hushed tones at home and told only a little less artfully. A book about Camp Dennison's history published in the mid-1950s mentions the patriarch of one of the first Black families to settle in the community. "George Walton, albeit a generous man, had grown tired of donating his free services to southern plantation owners, and had joined the Union army as a cook. At the war's end he found himself in Camp Dennison where he remained and reared his children," wrote Mary Rahn Sloan. While that first sentence makes me gag every time, much of the book is a gift. Sloan describes in detail a bustling and largely integrated town of around 600 people and a service station, grocery store, post office, active churches, and a tavern. Known in this house as "the beer garden," that tavern was across the street and is long gone, but my mom and her sisters still tell stories about the drunken shenanigans they could see from their bedroom windows.

Camp Dennison's unique history has become even more obscured in the twenty-five years between when I left for college and when a family health crisis brought me back to my childhood home last year. More white families have moved in as Black elders have sold their homes, often to young couples drawn by the promise of access to Indian Hill schools. While my childhood memories are of a neighborhood that was roughly half Black and half white, the most recent census data puts white residents at 80 percent. At the same time that the community has shifted from racially integrated to predominantly white, it's also shifting from an offbeat and remote enclave to something more like a typical east-side suburb. Growing up, I experienced Camp Dennison as distinctly rural. Unless we were on SR 126, which we called "the highway," we rode our bikes and walked down the middle of the street, confident that the infrequently passing cars would yield to us. We learned to fish on the wooded banks of the Little Miami. Our parents and grandparents tended to vegetable gardens in their spacious yards. Some of us have a country drawl I've never heard elsewhere, despite my far-flung travels. Whenever I hear my full first name pronounced "Dane-yell," I know I'm home.

These days, when I tell a fellow Cincinnatian where I live, they've usually heard of my neighborhood. That's in part because the Loveland Bike Trail is a destination for weekend warriors from all over the region. I remember when that same path through Camp Dennison was a faint dirt trail that marked what was left of the Little Miami Railroad, which was built in the late 1830s to connect Cincinnati to Springfield. As kids, we walked that path, seeking out adventures in the natural world. We called it "the tracks," though it didn't denote a divide between Black and white or rich and poor the way it often does in neighborhoods' social geographies. Now "the tracks" is one section of a seventy-mile ribbon of asphalt that carries speed demons outfitted in the latest Tour de France-inspired fashions between Lebanon and Newtown.

There's also Grand Valley, a nature preserve established on land purchased by Indian Hill in 2002. The 379-acre expanse stretches between SR 126 and the Little Miami at the northern reaches of Camp Dennison. It's where my grandfather and other men of his generation who lived here made their living, extracting the pebbles from the land and preparing them for commercial use. A new neighbor, a young woman with two kids, kept referring to all the fun they were having at "Grand Valley," and I just kept smiling and nodding, unsure what she was referring to. It has been and will always be the gravel pit to me. As Camp Dennison residents, we have access, as do people who live in Indian Hill. I recently used my mother's pass to access the gated preserve for the first time. There I saw many intrepid white people in canoes and on paddle boards. They fished, walked their dogs, or jogged along the peaceful pathways.

I don't begrudge these folks their leisure. I enjoy teaching my five-year-old to roller skate on the bike trail and skip stones on the lake down in the post-makeover gravel pit. But it's the entitlement displayed by many of these newcomers that gets me. Men on expensive bikes shout to each other as they travel in packs on the trail, seemingly oblivious to the quiet homes they're whizzing past. People with huge water toys strapped to the roofs of the cars drive by, undoubtedly readying the passes that will raise the gate to Grand Valley and grant them exclusive access to what used to be a blue-collar work site. Do they know this history? Do they care? Athleticism and a desire for adventure bring these visitors into a community that was here long before they discovered its bucolic beauty. I grieve the disappearance of the weird hidden gem we used to be. I anticipate even more change, and, as always, letting go of the past hurts.

SOUTH

Covington: The End of an Era at City Heights

BRIANA RICE

Some of my youngest years were spent in Covington. But not the Covington that all my friends are moving to now.

We lived in the subsidized housing projects known as City Heights, or as we called it, the Hill, at first.

We're a big family with some deep roots here. My great-grandma moved to Covington from Virginia. My grandma had eight siblings here. My dad had eleven. I have ten.

Of my dad's eleven siblings, one died, one owned a house in Covington, and the rest lived in City Heights at the same time as us. Grandma Betty lived a few houses down. Everyone I knew on my dad's side of the family was nearby or stopped by often.

Most of us have stayed in the area. It's a big deal if you've even made it across the river to Cincinnati.

City Heights—currently home to more than 762 people—is full of redbrick apartments built in the 1950s that all look the same. I was once playing outside with another little girl when I asked who her daddy was and found out that we were actually second cousins, our fathers first cousins.

"You're a Rice?!" people would say to me. My last name came with assumptions. There were so many of us, and we're known for getting into trouble.

We had everything we needed on the hill, with our little corner store full of snacks and a playground nearby.

There was a big field in the middle of the apartments that we could play in. We had to be close enough that we could hear my mom when she shouted for us.

The thing about northern Kentucky for the people who grew up there is that it really felt like we were all the same. In our Covington, we all knew each other and looked out for each other.

I remember my older brother telling me that people get shot in Cincinnati, that it was unsafe because there weren't as many people to call on that you knew.

But my mom thought things were better in Cincinnati, and so we were always enrolled in elementary schools across the river.

My mom was young. She had me a month before she turned twenty. But she was always concerned about our education. Everyone I knew was poor, full of blended families that had white kids and Black kids and Latina kids, cousins who were now siblings and kids who didn't have parents who watched them.

Our Covington expanded when I was nine and we moved to East Sixteenth Street. It was our first house, our first time not in an apartment with neighbors close by. It had two floors.

Our apartment in City Heights really only had a living room and a small kitchen to hang out in. Now we had a yard and space to all sit down together at a table.

Though we now had four bedrooms, my siblings and I still preferred to sleep piled on top of each other in one room. Though this new house was less than ten minutes from our old apartment, it felt like a new world.

City Heights sits on top of a big hill that we were not allowed to leave and probably would not have considered doing. Once we moved into the "city," my mom finally let us start heading out on our own.

On the street behind us was a trailer park community full of kids. Around the corner was a man who lived alone and was always having kittens and puppies for us to come visit.

My mom didn't have to watch us as much anymore. We biked blocks and blocks throughout Covington, sometimes picking up kids and friends along the way. We were older; there were more spaces to play in, more places to go.

Sometimes we'd ride to the park at Sixth District Elementary School. It was one of those wooden nineties ones that reminded you of a castle. I was afraid of the slides because some older kids told me they had sex there. One time while playing in the sand, a fishhook went into my finger.

But most of the time it was fun. We were the Code Name Kids Next Door. The Teen Titans. Avatar the Last Air Bender.

In the summer, there were two pools near our house. For some reason, at the bigger one, someone would always poop, and we'd be stuck in the sun for an hour while they cleaned.

We did all the free things. The camps. The lunches. We went down to the riverfront, played on the slides and the hills.

I had four younger siblings to look after at the time and whatever friends and cousins came along for the ride.

No one ever bothered us in our Covington. Even when there were ten kids riding through the streets, playing loudly—whoever's parents were nearest kept us in line. We didn't have phones for my mom to check on us, but we never got lost.

My Covington isn't the Covington that everyone thinks of now. One of my friends just moved into a new building on Mainstrasse, and people take me out for dinner and drinks around there.

So many of the buildings are new. It doesn't feel like the Covington I remember. Most everyone is white.

The local housing authority is selling City Heights—one of the first places that my young mother could make a home for all of us—and telling residents there they must leave.

When I drive through Covington, away from Madison and Mainstrasse, one of my childhood pools is still there. The Frank Duveneck Arts and Cultural Center where I took some of my first free writing classes is still standing.

I'm twenty-five now, and after years of saving, my mom and dad were able to buy a home of their own in 2020. It's in a suburb on the west side of Cincinnati. Most of my aunties and uncles got to leave City Heights and found better homes. Most had to leave Covington to do so. There weren't many affordable options when I was young, and it's only gotten more expensive.

The kids I grew up with are now having kids of their own, looking for housing of their own. We aren't looking in Covington. We can't afford it.

Ludlow: Grounded by the River

KATRINA ERESMAN

After my parents divorced, my mom couldn't stop moving. That was seven years ago. Since then, we've had family dinners in seven different zip codes. My brother and I moved her things into quaint, little houses, suburban condos with sliding door patios, two-story townhouses with deer in the backyard.

The last time she moved, she announced it in an email signed, "your crazy, real estate buying mom." That was almost two years ago, and I think she's staying put.

Her most recent move was to Ludlow, Kentucky, a little town on the Ohio River across from Cincinnati's western extremities. Before incorporating during the height of the Civil War in 1864, the land Ludlow sits on was passed between several owners. At one point, a British entertainer named William Bullock had the idea to turn the land into a utopian settlement named "Hygeia."

Hygeia never happened, and Ludlow developed in its place. Although Ludlow may fall a little short of utopian, it's pleasant enough for the estimated 4,500 people who live there.

Mom's house is a two-story structure from the early 1900s that sits on a corner across from a lumberyard. My mom bought it from a young married couple with a German shepherd puppy who needed more outdoor space. They had completely renovated the house, saving it from a decrepit state. Every detail—the open kitchen, the restored Rookwood tile, the shiplap stairwell—was to their taste.

A week or two after the move, I was standing on a ladder in my mom's living room, helping her put books onto the built-in shelves. She told me the couple had called her and asked that she reach out to them should she ever consider selling. The wife missed the place. It was their first home as a couple, and she wanted it back.

But there was no going backward. All of us—the young couple, the German shepherd, my family—were building new homes.

I've set an intention to know Ludlow like I knew my childhood neighborhood. I don't just want to memorize its streets—I want to know the way the sun feels walking down one side of the road versus the other. I want to learn the names of people who have lived there forever, to remember the houses with the best spring gardens. This is what I need, for my sake and for my mother's. Part of us has been uprooted, and we need coherency. We'll find it through Ludlow.

Ludlow's proximity to the river is one of its best features. Before I knew Ludlow, I knew the Ludlow-Bromley Yacht Club, a floating bar and grill on the edge of the Ohio River. In late 2019, a barge ran into the restaurant and demolished it.

The owners of the devastated Yacht Club have expressed their determination to reopen their floating community. But for now, they direct their devout customers to the Lagoon Saloon, which is situated safely on land.

Before its demise, my mom would take me there to have beers and appetizers on the river. We would sit under the sprawling, red Budweiser umbrellas, her with a Heineken and me with a Blue Moon. She devotes herself to places that she loves, and the Ludlow-Bromley Yacht Club was one of those.

Another Ludlow landmark that had her heart was the Folk School Coffee Parlor. Before its closing, it provided access to all things folk music—history, instrument lessons, live performances. My mom took advantage of all the offerings. She keeps the washboard she played in her group lesson in the trunk of her car, should there ever be a last-minute jam requiring additional percussion.

The Folk School Coffee Parlor sign is still up above its door on Elm Street. When my mom and I walk past, she tends to reminisce about the times she went to see Jerry Springer record his podcast in there, which he started doing in 2015. Somewhere on the internet she has posted a terrible photo of me, my brother, and Jerry, posing stiffly in the back of the coffeehouse.

Ludlow is tiny and walkable, and this is how we explore it. Elm Street draws a line almost parallel to the Ohio River, from Bromley on the west end to Covington on the east. Devou Park's amorphous shape defines the southern border of Ludlow. The park is technically part of Covington, but some of its trails dip into Ludlow for easy access.

The one park that Ludlow can officially claim as its own is Ludlow Memorial Park. It's small and rectangular and right along the river. There are no hiking trails and no woods, but there is a playground, basketball courts, and a skatepark.

I started park skating with a pair of old roller derby skates in 2020. When my mom moved to Ludlow, we both noted the proximity of the skate park. I envisioned wholesome postskate hangouts, complete with snacks and beer. On one unseasonably warm day the winter after her move, we went to check it out.

There's no paved pathway leading from the sidewalk to the skate park—as one miffed, two-star Google review will have you know. The road ends at a gravel lot behind a baseball diamond. I stomped across the loose stones and the adjacent field with my skates on. Once we arrived at the skate park, I rolled up and down the rusty ramps while my mom took videos on her phone, engrossed as only a mother could be.

It's a quick walk to the park from my mom's house. Everything in Ludlow is a quick walk from anywhere. Our habit, of late, is to take a straight shot down her street toward Elm. Before Elm, we pass by houses with small yards, sometimes dogs, and often neighbors sitting outside on their porches. On the other side of Elm, she points out a gorgeous brick home that belongs to an old friend from her days in radio. We take our time admiring the big houses in this nook of the neighborhood, including Somerset Hall, a huge, Greek Revival-style home from the 1840s.

I remember picking out my favorite houses in our neighborhood when I was a kid. The practice breeds a sense of ownership and familiarity. It gives you a conversation piece on your bike rides with friends. On our walk, I try to imagine which of them would have stood out to me when I was little. Possibly the one with fifteen solar-powered dancing flowers in the window.

Sometimes our walks are just to see the river. Other times we end them with a meal. With the Yacht Club and her folk haven shut down, my mom was quick to find another local spot to support. Almost as soon as she moved in, she became a regular at Taste on Elm, a small gourmet grocery store specializing in wine and cheese. Its sidewalk cafe seating was our first meal out during the pandemic. We each ordered a glass of wine and a sandwich from the panini menu. I think often of my selection, an understated stack of salami, garlic pickles, and pimento cheese.

My mom might say she's there for the sandwiches, but I know the real selling point for her is the owner, a chatty woman named Lauren. In order to feel at home in a place, you need community, someone expecting you here or there. I'd never really seen my mom drink wine pre-Ludlow. Now she's always picking up bottles just to say hello to her neighborhood sommelier.

Most of my mom's neighbors are still strangers to her. She moved during the pandemic, so opportunities for mingling were scarce. But sometime during that first year there, she heard loud music playing down the street. When she investigated, she was greeted by a friendly stranger, one of many gathered for a block party. They were celebrating, he said, in memory of someone who lived on the block. The stranger introduced himself and invited her to join in on the memorial and meet the other neighbors.

My mom graciously declined, feeling odd about memorializing someone she didn't know. Still, she explained later, she was uplifted by the notion that her neighbors cared for one another.

With every move, my mom went through the checklist. She changed her mailing address, memorized the best route to the grocery store, and hung up her artwork. But settling in and belonging to a place is more abstract than simple logistics. It is achieved by familiar faces, preferred sunset views, favorite sandwiches. You have to find the nuances that make you feel like more than a visitor.

My mom knows, for instance, that the best sunset view is through her kitchen window. She likes the way it disappears behind the black silhouette of a Ludlow church steeple. Sometimes I'm there when it happens, and we watch together at the kitchen counter. I sense a stillness in these moments, a satisfaction she hadn't been able to find in her other quarters. Knowing this, I feel a little more grounded. I think she may have found her spot.

Bellevue:
Heaven in Bellevue
CAITLYN SHORT

Bellevue was never my home, but it is home to my grandmother's spirit.

Her likeness remains in every friendly face that shines upon me when I stroll down Sixth Avenue, which divides the little downtown in half.

The smell of Fessler's Pizza and the sound of the bell on the door ringing each time its opened in Schneider's Sweets Shop evoke memories of when my grandmother brought me down each time she was due for a salon visit at Joann's Hairstylings.

We would pile into her car and listen to the vocal stylings of the McGuire Sisters, Martha Reeves, and Bobby Darin as we trekked from Milford, Ohio, down to the little river town in Kentucky.

The visit was always to visit my grandmother's only known place of worship to me: Joann's.

Her little red Buick acted as a time machine, and as we entered Bellevue, it took us back to the days of soda fountains, milkmen, and *Leave It to Beaver*. We would pull up alongside Joann's, and I could smell the scent of Elnett Satin hairspray as we hopped out of the car.

This little cross section of streets was the nexus of my grandmother's universe.

Bellevue, which has been around since about 1870 and is now home to about 6,000 folks, was nothing like my hometown of Milford. Here, people walked their dogs in town and said hello to each other with a smile. You could see unattended kids walking into Schneider's for a piece of candy or peanut butter fudge. On hot summer days, the line into Schneider's would stretch around the corner as kids would debate about which scoop of ice cream they were going to get in their waffle cone.

You could see the mighty Ohio River barreling by from Joann's front stoop, and sometimes folks would be headed that way for a stroll with a kite or a bicycle or fishing pole in hand. To me, this was the town of Mayberry from my mother's favorite show brought to life.

Once we were inside Joann's, the sounds of women chatting were layered with the soap operas on the television and an undercurrent of wax strips being pulled and UV tubes buzzing in the tanning room down the hall.

I would sit in the chairs in front as the women in the shop peppered Grandma Bettye with questions about my parents, my brother, and myself. My grandma was everyone's best friend, and a lot of the women in the shop adored her as much as our own family did. I'd flip through 1980s hair magazines while they laughed and caught up.

While my grandma knew everyone here, the only one she entrusted with her bouffant-style hair was Joann herself. Joann was a small woman who wore tall slingback heels and had dark tanned skin. Joann made you feel like you were the only one in the salon when she spoke to you and like you were the funniest person she had ever met.

Even as a child, I knew Joann was special, and she made my sweet Grandma Bettye feel special too. That's what they were both good at, making others feel like they were the center of their world. And when my grandma got sick the second time around, Joann was the only person who could make her laugh out loud.

The salon had the interior decorating stylings of heaven itself. Clouds and cherubs were hand-painted on every wall, and angel statues dotted every shelf. When I was very small, I believed heaven could be found right there on Sixth Avenue.

Once my grandma's hair was properly dyed and coiffed, it was my turn to sit in the chair. Joann would run her long, painted fingernails through my blonde hair and ask me about school and boys. One day when I was either five or six, I asked about hot curlers and she obliged, taking every strand and lovingly wrapping it around each curler.

I wanted to feel grown up and sit underneath the large iron hat all the adults got to wear around their heads in their service. She removed the curls and I exclaimed, "I look like George Washington!" Joann laughed and told me I'd have to suffer looking like George for a day.

After a successful salon visit, we would walk two blocks to Fessler's for some pizza. My grandma is still the only person I've ever encountered who could say "the usual" in answer to "What will you have?" by any establishment and have them understand exactly what she meant.

That usual was a medium half-cheese, half-pepperoni pizza, a small salad with Italian dressing, garlic bread with cheese, and a hoagie to go for my grandpa at home. I remember sitting in a chair in Fessler's, in awe at how everybody knew everybody and got along.

We'd cap our visits to Bellevue with a trip to Schneider's. I'd get a scoop of rainbow sherbet and my grandma a scoop of vanilla. Even at Schneider's, my grandma was known by name.

As I got older, the salon seemed to get smaller, as did the town it sat in. Even as a teenager in high school, I'd still ride in my grandma's car over to Bellevue, singing along to the Shirelles' "Will You Love Me Tomorrow" and "Mama Said," with Grandma's hums as an accompanying duet. I finally got to partake in the sermons behind the big red walls of Joann's salons as we laughed and carried on with Joann and her stylists.

I don't remember the first time my grandma got cancer. I may have been too young to understand. It must have been scary for my great big family of sixty members and the family my grandma created for herself in every place she went to—places like Bellevue. My grandma was a grandma, a mother, and at the very least a friend to just about everyone she met.

I do remember our last visit to Bellevue. We took the long route, and I changed the channel when Frank Sinatra's "It Was a Very Good Year" came over the airwaves, neither one of us wanting to get nostalgic for times gone by.

Instead, we opted for the lightness of Dee Dee Sharp instructing us to do the Mashed Potato. Somehow, I knew it was the last time I'd drive down Sixth Avenue with the soundtrack of my grandma's hums. We pulled up to Joann's and walked inside; ladies in their chairs noticed my grandma's scarf around her scalp and knew not to ask. They smiled and chatted like it was any other day. Joann took us back beyond the tanning beds into the little restroom. My grandma asked if I would wait outside. I obliged but could still hear remnants of the conversation. Joann mentioned something about her being able to hide what wasn't there. And my grandma, in tears, asking for help. I had never heard my grandma cry like that.

Together we walked out of heaven and into the red Buick time machine. This time, I was the pilot while Joann directed me to a wig shop nearby. There, laughs at first, Joann pulled down a bright purple bob and swayed my grandma to try it on. We finally settled on something Joann could "shape up" into the bouffant my grandma had known all her life.

Back in the salon, my grandma sat in Joann's chair for the last time. She winked at me, as she always did, from the chair beneath my favorite painted cherub. For a moment, we had a sense of normalcy as Joann joked around behind her. We couldn't help but visit our favorite spots just one more time, coming away with a little more peanut butter fudge and garlic bread than usual.

Joann passed away a few years after my grandma, leaving an angel-shaped hole on the corner of Sixth and Foote. Joann's salon is still there, though some time ago, they removed all the cherub and angel statues.

Even though Bellevue is much different now than it was twenty years ago, it still has that friendliness. You will still see kids lining up around the block to get into Schneider's, and you will still find someone picking up a hoagie over at Fessler's for a hungry person back home. The women are still showing up at Joann's door, ready to share some secrets over a bottle of toner and hairspray. Time still seems to move slower here on Sixth Avenue, while the sun still sets on the sparkling Ohio River, leaving Bellevue in a golden glow on the edge of heaven.

Newport: The Lost Story of a Workers' Strike

THURMAN WENZL

If we think of distant Newport history, we often think of the infamous organized crime the city was once known for: the gambling, sex, and booze that ended decades ago.

But there is also another history here, one in which workers pushed for more rights. A large strike in the steel mills took place on the west side of the city in the winter of 1921–1922, garnering some major support from the community—and also some outbreaks of violence.

Newport was already a relatively old city by that point. Established in 1795, the town grew slowly during the region's early years. By 1850, only about 1,000 people lived here—a big contrast with its neighbor Cincinnati across the river, which was by that time the sixth-largest city in the country with more than 115,000 people.

But the continued march of industrialization and early mass transit—in the form of mule-driven streetcars—expanded Newport's population significantly.

That expansion came in two flavors. Wealthy businessman and Kroger Grocery Company founder Barney Kroger was living on Newport's east side in an enormous mansion by the 1890s. Plenty of other well-to-do commuters at the time crossed the river every morning from the east side of Newport into downtown Cincinnati.

Meanwhile, the city's west side became its industrial hub. By the turn of the twentieth century, Newport was home to 134 manufacturers employing, on average, about fifteen people.

As the twentieth century wore on, those businesses consolidated down to forty-six companies, each employing an average of fifty-two workers by 1929.

All of this, combined with national pressures, pushed workers to organize. In December 1921, 2,500 workers at the Newport Rolling Mill went on strike.

This large mill had at least five open-hearth furnaces and had been in operation at least since 1867. Their products include galvanized steel roofing and corrugated piping for culverts. Workweeks of more than seventy hours were not unusual, sometimes with only a day off every two weeks. Much earlier in 1873, skilled workers had struck to protest a 10 percent pay cut.

The principal issues in the 1921 strikes were union recognition, namely the obligation of the company to bargain and the desire that all workers belong to the union. Wages and working conditions appear not to have been an issue.

The company insisted on an open shop. But the workers wanted unionization, and they weren't the only ones. The *Kentucky Post* wrote in an editorial in support of the workers, "This newspaper believes that the open shop is bad for workers but is also bad for the community."

Plenty of those living in Newport—especially its western half—were sympathetic to that cause.

In one example of widespread neighborhood support for unions, local women stopped a nonunion bread delivery man. They explained that even though the bread had a union label, they would not allow him to deliver it in their neighborhood since he did not belong to the Teamsters Union. That union was originally made up of men who drove teams of horses.

These striking workers were in the Amalgamated Association of Iron, Steel, and Tin Workers (AA), which had grown into a large craft union during the war years (1917–1919), when demand for steel was high and the Wilson administration was not opposed to workers organizing. The AA grew with the use of member organizers, as they did not have the resources to send out staff organizers from their headquarters in Pittsburgh.

But political tides shifted, and the early 1920s were not friendly to workers organizing. This was a period of repression, with so-called Palmer Raids by the federal government occurring against activists in many parts of the country. One national strike took place later in 1922: all the railway shopmen (mechanics) struck around the country, including in Corbin, Kentucky, where community support was complete. Eventually, this strike was lost due to government repression and a lack of support from other unions.

Back in Newport, Newport Steel responded to the community support for the strikers by erecting no fewer than thirty-six machine guns and searchlights on their mill, which they claimed were needed in case the plant was attacked. The company occasionally used these guns, and there was some striker violence against scabs—although one union leader, John Williams, reported that the union was urging its members to abstain from violence, and that most shooting was being initiated by the company.

Disagreement continued about who was responsible for violence on the picket lines, and in one case, a strike supporter (identified as an umbrella mender) was arrested for refusing an order to "move on" from a militia member. He had a jury trial for "breach of the peace" and was found not guilty by a jury that was even identified by name in the article. Later, a "mill guard was arrested and charged with carrying a concealed weapon—based on a complaint by striking workers."

After the company realized that the Newport police were not doing enough to curb the pickets, they appealed to the governor to send in the state militia, which he did. The company also sought a temporary restraining order from the Campbell County Court, which, among other things, restricted the strikers to just two picketers at each entrance to the mill.

The community was not thrilled about the militia, and a state representative from Newport, Herman Thompson, called for an investigation into the reasons for sending in the troops; the company opposed such an investigation. A local druggist was quoted as saying that he had "suffered untold indignities at the hands of the militia."

Neither of these steps had the desired effect, as the militia commander was quoted as upholding the rights of the strikers, and the soldiers confiscated the machine guns that the company had installed.

The state militia commander, Col H. H. Denhardt, apparently had conflicting loyalties. At one point on January 4, he reportedly gave orders to "shoot to kill." But later, on January 8, he was quoted thus by the *Kentucky Post*: "I am a friend of union labor because I believe in collective bargaining. Workmen have a right to organize for that purpose."

The militia built wooden barracks within the steel mill and stayed more than four months.

A community committee made up of religious and other leaders tried to bring the workers and company together for a just and fair settlement. But steel mill officials refused to negotiate. And in a January 11 editorial, the *Kentucky Post* again commented in support of the strikers, opining that "the workers' right to collective bargaining cannot any longer be considered arbitrable."

The women of the neighborhood continued to be actively involved, with a "Sew for Strikers" campaign that resulted in the formation of the Women's Volunteer Relief Committee. Their plan, which attracted fifty volunteers, was to have a card party to raise funds for strikers' families.

One *Kentucky Post* headline screamed "IWW Threat Seen," speculating that outside activists from the Industrial Workers of the World had arrived and were planning sabotage against the mill. The paper went on to report that the local strike committee was not happy about these visitors, reporting that "several strangers, believed to be members of that organization, were ordered away from the strike zone by union pickets."

After a month of stalemate with continued community support for the strikers, Kentucky governor Edwin Morrow visited Newport in an attempt to negotiate a settlement. He met with local and union officials and the company, but the company would not budge on the principal demand for union recognition.

After a few months, the strike was lost, workers drifted back into the mill, and many of the union leaders had to move away to seek similar jobs in nearby cities. About fifteen years later, with the New Deal resurgence of industrial unions, the workers chose to be represented by the United Steel Workers of America.

Much more recently, parts of the mill moved to Wilder, and the operations in west Newport ceased. The pipe mill still operates in Wilder, now owned by a Russian corporation.

NORTH

Carthage: Four Cultures, Four Congregations

REV. ALAN DICKEN

My grandparents met between the squeaky wooden pews of the old church on Seventy-Third and Fairpark. Though I think the carpeting was added much later, I imagine that the small sanctuary looked much the same then as it does now. All those years ago, under ornate lighting fixtures and between simple stained-glass windows, as the church bell rang out throughout the neighborhood, a young man and a young woman met. This neighborhood and this church mean a lot to our family.

Carthage Christian Church has sat in that spot since 1879, though the neighborhood congregation has existed since 1832. It took two fires before the building would take up its permanent residence. Up until last year, I had the honor of serving as the pastor. Although I have been called to another ministry, I will always think fondly of the first church I served just out of seminary.

I loved walking the halls and looking at the artwork. In the basement, there's a photograph of my grandfather shaking hands with the minister. At the time, he was a trustee, and I have to believe that his plaid suit jacket must have made sense during that era.

A little further down the wall, there's an old painting that depicts a church in the woods. It is this church. The painting doesn't show the road or the sidewalks that border the grounds now. Instead, the viewer sees a simple forest scene, with a gathered community presumably just arriving for service on Sunday morning. Since its founding, at least two people have taken communion there every Sunday. Even after those fires. Even through snowstorms and amidst a pandemic rivaled only by that of the 1917 flu. The church has seen a lot.

The old brick building with a small steeple pointing heavenward has served more than just the Sunday morning crowd. It is a place where folks can come to participate in the neighborhood civic league, the Carthage seniors' curse-laden games of "chair-volleyball," Halloween parties, Easter egg hunts, prostitution call-ins, anti-human-trafficking services, Black Lives Matter meetings, protest vigils, music and arts camps, free concerts where

CCM students play for a neighborhood that doesn't always get to hear live music, quinceañeras, after-school tutoring lessons, baby showers, weddings, funerals, and so, so, so many meals.

My family has been connected to this neighborhood and this church for generations. Many others have as well. Carthage has been described as "Urban Appalachia," a term that only makes sense if you have both been to Carthage and have your own roots somewhere in the hills of eastern Kentucky or even West Virginia. One family spread out across a single street, with Ma and Pa across the street. A couple houses down the way are where some aunts and uncles live, and you're always just a couple of doors down from Granny's.

Over the years, the families that settled in Carthage grew and changed, and so too did the neighborhood. The Carthage Fairgrounds became the Hamilton County Fairgrounds as the agricultural area shifted toward urban sprawl and the city grew northward. The Hamilton County Fairgrounds stand there today and are home to demolition derbies, maker's fairs, flea markets, and Hispanic Fest.

Some of the old-timers still sit on the front porch and talk about how Vine Street was a thriving business district before I-75 clawed its way parallel to the previously busy thoroughfare. Folks still use the drive-through on Vine to pick up a six-pack, and whenever you go past it, you point at Andy's pub and say that former Speaker of the House John Boehner used to sweep the floors there. It's a different bar now with different owners, but the name remains the same.

The neighborhood of Urban Appalachia and blue-collar white workers slowly became more diverse. Black families started living across the street from white families, but the big shift came when the Catholic diocese decreed that St. Charles would become San Carlos. Carthage now has welcome signs in English and Spanish. Valle Verde lies at the southern tip of Carthage, and you can get the most delicious and most authentic Central American food in the entire city of Cincinnati. These neighbors have been great for Carthage.

It isn't just the businesses that show the neighborhood for what it is though. Not too long ago, there was a line of congregations down Fairpark Avenue that you might not expect to see on a Sunday morning.

New Jerusalem Baptist Church stands strong and blocky with its fiery preacher, Rev. Damon Lynch Jr., the civil rights leader and icon in the city, giving a good word to scores of Black families up on Fairpark and North Bend.

Head south and you're back to the little sanctuary from the start of our story. Carthage Christian Church is a small but progressive congregation with a rainbow flag out front and a proud welcome of the LGBTQIA+ community.

Not long ago, you'd have also run into San Carlos Catholic Church. *Si quieres escuchar tus sermones en español, esta es la iglesia para ti.* Hundreds of Spanish-speaking immigrants walk to their neighborhood church to receive the mass and the blessings of Father Rodolfo.

A little further down and you'll find a congregation of Nigerian immigrants led by Rev. Isaiah Ojo. What a beautiful Sunday morning, with people wearing exactly what they would wear if they were at church in Nigeria. You can hear the singing of beautiful songs for hours on end.

Just four blocks and you see four cultures in four congregations. And every Thanksgiving, with the addition of the Church of the Nazarene, we did a community service together. We brought our choirs, sang songs from our cultures, prayed in our own languages, and together, we raised money for the local food pantry housed at the little brick church.

All of this sounds like history, and that's because Carthage has a lot of history to share. But it's also because the tall spire of San Carlos can no longer be seen jutting up into the sky. New businesses are opening up, more neighbors are moving in, the civic league has been working on improvement plans with the city, and the neighborhood continues to change.

The small church with the bricks wrinkled from age still stands though. And even though I no longer serve as the pastor, the seven years when I did helped me to reconnect with this neighborhood and the faiths found here. As Carthage evolves, I wonder if I'll ever see a painting of how the church stands now and think about how odd it looks surrounded by telephone wires and cars parked on the street. Maybe more trees will grow back. I wonder if my own grandchildren will come one day, point at a photo of me in my out-of-date fashions, and say, "Grandfather used to preach here, and his grandparents met here. Yes, this neighborhood and this church mean a lot to our family."

Northside: Honeysuckle and Urban Streams

KATIE VOGEL

The most attractive aspect of Northside isn't its tongue-in-cheek Fourth of July parade that features a posse of women doing kick lines with lawn chairs. It's not the intriguing mix of housing stock, ranging from Italianate masterpieces to currently-under-construction senior housing. It's not even the hilarity of our neighborhood Facebook group, which serves as a place to be notified when your chicken breaks out of her yard and goes for a walk.

It's the accessibility of nature and the calm gathering of my neighbors around conservation and restoration in a time of increasing divisions in our world.

I can step out my door and with a short walk, be deep in the ravine of a nature preserve or watching herons congregate along an urban stream. These walks sometimes lead to encounters with neighbors and friends, but more often than not, they are solo affairs that allow for quietude.

In a neighborhood defined by close social ties, solitude is a precious, imagined commodity.

During the early stages of the pandemic, my occasional walks through Buttercup Valley Preserve turned into a routine that removed me from the loop of doom-scrolling that had come to define daily life. Whatever storm might be brewing on Twitter in April 2020 had nothing on the emergence of tiny Dutchmen's breeches and extravagant trillium on the forest floor. That spring, the sharp scent of garlic from a patch of ramps reminded me how much I missed the simple pleasure of sharing a pizza with friends on Saturday nights.

While there were moments of longing for company, of missing hugs from friends, and of missing feasts on festival days, there wasn't a moment where I regretted being in those woods by myself. Sycamores tower over the rest of the canopy. A small marsh is studded with jewel weed that springs open at the slightest touch. A few steps in and you're swallowed up by a tunnel of greenery that quickly silences the noise of city life.

It is a challenge to hear the distant thrum of cars on I-75, but it is never hard to hear the raucous community of woods creatures. They are occupied in a never-ending deafening shouting match to defend territory, find love, and share the latest gossip. "Wocka-wocka-wocka!" scream pileated woodpeckers. Not to be outdone, the deafening cry of "TEAKETTLE! TEAKETTLE! TEAKETTLE" erupts from impossibly tiny Carolina wrens. Emerging from the woods onto the street, a mockingbird reminds its neighbors that we're still in the city with a perfect imitation of the signature "beep BEEP" of a small sedan's locking alarm.

In Northside, nature is healing, in an unironic, extremely offline kind of way.

Recently, these woods had been overrun by invasive honeysuckle, once prized by gardeners for its hardiness and sweet scent. It crowded out the vistas and choked the tiny wildflowers that now seemed to explode across the forest floor. But this terrible shrub continues to be eradicated, thanks to a dedicated group of volunteers who have mindfully, gleefully hacked down the invasive monster and then bathed its stumps in glyphosate, a chemical guaranteed to prevent the regrowth of this stubborn plant. (No, there's really not a better way to kill it.)

The explosive growth of honeysuckle, and the necessity of human intervention to contain this fast-spreading ornamental shrub, is a painfully obvious (and structurally lazy) metaphor for the messiness of humanity and our tendency to make terrible decisions. We had massively screwed up by being lax custodians of our own backyard shrubs, which had escaped the confines of our domesticated bits of lawn. But instead of accepting the destruction of an urban woodland, here were these merry bands of volunteers, roving the steep slopes of the ravines, armed with saws and chemicals and a shared understanding that these terrible shrubs needed to die.

As a result of this scorched-earth campaign, freshly cleared hillsides were quickly covered with a misty shroud of olive-colored native plants. It offered up a real-time vision of the kind of transformation that can take place with deep commitment and a certain finesse with pruning shears.

It's a heartening lesson Northside's nature and its people offer up: Change is possible. Restoration can happen. People can work together.

A twenty-minute walk down the valley, another army of volunteers and nonprofits have engaged in an extraordinary cleanup of an urban stream. The Mill Creek winds down toward the Ohio River. Osprey and kingfishers and colonies of night herons can now be found on any given day on a waterway that was once treated as an open-dumping ground for sewage, industrial runoff, and seemingly every unwanted tire and shopping cart in the tri-state area.

In 1997, the Mill Creek was named North America's "most endangered urban river." Less than three decades later, the bloodworms that thrive in low-oxygen water laden with untreated sewage are gone. The chittering of kingfishers diving to scoop up minnows may be drowned out by semitrucks on I-75, but there they are, multiplying on this waterway that was once a poster child of pollution and misplaced priorities.

"Nature" as we think of it, is often a fabrication. It's how we imagine the woods and the streams (and the rivers they pour into) and how we tame them to be accessible and inviting. It's not the terror of true wilderness. It's domesticated. It's approachable. It's (probably) not going to kill us. But it's something we've constructed, tended to, abused, ignored, and repaired.

It's easy to talk about Northside as an eclectic mix of businesses or as a diverse and quirky community. It's harder to talk about our disparities and ugly bits and the darker insinuations we're willing to weaponize when we talk about one another online. But perhaps by stepping into the loudness or the woods, or up to the bank of a creek teeming with life and buzzing with the sounds of interstate traffic, we can begin to move beyond imagining our community and our place within it and reckon with the place we've built and create the place we want it to become.

College Hill: Big in Abolition, Big in Japan

GAIL FINKE

College Hill has been home to tough pioneers, daring abolitionists, a world-famous inventor, and several long-vanished colleges. People who come from the neighborhood have changed the world, at least a little bit.

That might surprise those who know the northern Cincinnati neighborhood was incorporated in 1866 for its tree-lined streets and neat rows of sometimes stately homes.

And there are stories even many residents don't know, including one about the extraordinary friendship of two women that made College Hill well known in Japan.

Etsuko Inagaki was born in 1874 to a powerful feudal family that was ruined soon after her birth by the Meiji Restoration, which ended feudalism in Japan. Etsu, as she was called, moved to College Hill in 1898 to marry a man she had never met: Matsunosuke Sugimoto, owner of a Japanese import store.

Educated by Methodist missionaries and a convert to Christianity, Etsu wrote later that her teachers had shown her a new way to think that enabled her to lead a different life from most Japanese women of the time. The couple were married in the College Hill summer home of Obed Wilson, a prominent Methodist and publisher, where they lived for eight years. Obed's niece Florence was maid of honor at the wedding, and the older woman took Etsu under her wing, first as a substitute mother and then as a lifelong friend who helped her become a best-selling writer.

Florence moved to Japan with Etsu for a year's visit, then stayed to live the vanishing life of the feudal Japanese for a year without her. She eventually sold her American property to return to Japan with Etsu after Matsuo's early death. The friends moved back and forth from Japan until Florence's death in 1932, and each woman was an informal ambassador for the other's country and culture.

Florence helped Etsu rewrite an autobiographical novel of her life after a publisher rejected it, and in 1925, *A Daughter of the Samurai* was a best-seller in the United States and Europe. When Florence died in 1932, her ashes were interred in Tokyo's Aoyama Cemetery. Years later, Etsu's ashes were interred in a monument next to that of her "life-long Mother-Friend." The women's friendship has been explored in books and a 2015 Japanese documentary film.

Pioneering spirit and social reform, often combined with strong religious faith, have been a hallmark of College Hill residents rich and poor since its founding shortly after the American Revolution. Like Thomas Jefferson, its founders envisioned a future of "gentlemen farmers," and its earliest residents had farms *and* held state or national office: William Cary, who helped plat the original village and became one of its largest landowners, was an Ohio legislator and noted abolitionist; his son Samuel Fenton Cary was a US congressman, candidate for vice president, and leader of the Sons of Temperance, as well as a founder of the College Hill Presbyterian Church.

Other faith-filled leaders include circuit-riding Methodist preacher Danforth Witherby, who built a well in 1799 that's the area's oldest standing structure, and Freeman Grant Cary (another son of William), who founded Farmers' College in the 1840s to educate the sons of farmers to lead the young nation. Cary brought Robert Hamilton Bishop from Miami University to be its president. A Presbyterian minister from Scotland, Bishop had clashed with Miami over abolition (the university favored states' rights), and under his leadership, Farmers' College became a haven for abolitionists and a stop on the Underground Railroad.

John Witherspoon Scott, another abolitionist who came to Farmers' College from Miami, later founded the Ohio Female College, and he hid fugitive slaves in his home. Future US President Benjamin Harrison would have been a Farmers College alumnus if the women's college, the fifth in the nation, hadn't moved from College Hill to Oxford—he transferred to Miami to be close enough to woo Scott's daughter, Caroline.

Another faith-filled reformer and gentleman farmer associated with the colleges was Rabbi Isaac Mayer Wise, one of the founders of Reform Judaism. He bought a farm of his own in what is now North College Hill so his children could attend, and later founded Hebrew Union College in Clifton. Later, such reformers include Dr. John Willke, founder of numerous Right to Life organizations, whose busy Hamilton Avenue home office saw College Hill families for decades; and longtime College Hill Presbyterian Church pastor Rev. Jerry Kirk, founder of Citizens for Community Values (now the Center for Civic Virtue). In the 1960s, neighborhood ministers banded together to help combat "white flight" and foster understanding among its now-racially and economically diverse population; their work helped make College Hill remain one of the city's most integrated residential communities.

College Hill School principal Harriet Wilson documented the neighborhood's Underground Railroad history. Her family participated, along with college faculty, students, and neighbors. Escaped slaves were hidden in wagons brought up the steep Hamilton Avenue toll road from Cincinnati, and they were secreted in ravines behind the tollhouse until they could be driven north. One local Union soldier, John T. Crawford, escaped Libby Prison in Richmond, Virginia, and walked home, aided along the way by both slaves and free Black laborers. He left his entire estate on North Bend Road to found "an asylum and home for aged and worthy colored men" that operated from 1888 until it combined with a home in Walnut Hills in the 1960s.

Other notable residents include inventor Powell Crosley Jr., who graduated from the Ohio Military Institute (on the grounds of the old Farmers' College) and later started what became WLW in his College Hill bedroom; eight-term Cincinnati councilman and ambassador to Liberia Jesse Locker, who grew up here and was valedictorian of College Hill High School; photographer Paul Briol; and illustrator Caroline Wilson.

The house Etsu and Matsuo lived in is long gone—the Wilsons later donated the entire property to the Methodist Home for the Aged (now Twin Towers—renowned architect Samuel Hannaford donated the plans). Long gone too are most of the mansions and their famed grounds, the Farmers College model farm, the glamorous hotel and restaurant at the top of the Hamilton Avenue streetcar line, the military academy and its daily parades and canon shoot, and the water tower that tempted sightseers to climb the winding metal stairs to the highest point in Hamilton County. But College Hill is still growing, still a place of innovation—and still big in Japan.

Forest Park/Fairfield: The Death and Life of American Malls

RONNY SALERNO

I'm not the only person with a personal perspective on the cavernous and mostly empty mall that stands just off Cincinnati's ring highway, I-275, between the northern suburbs of Forest Park and Fairfield.

It's technically called "Forest Fair Village," though all the signs still say "Cincinnati Mall," that name itself a quick rebrand from "Cincinnati Mills."

I can wax nostalgic about the original arcade, the former Ferris wheel, the miniature golf, both former cinemas, and the various generations of stores with the best of them. I cashed in my "Book-It" certificates for free personal pan pizzas at the food court Pizza Hut, biked to Media Play to purchase *Tony Hawk's Pro Skater 2*, watched a girl brutally dump a guy when I was first figuring out what love was, and heard all the eye-roll-inducing, pearl-clutching suburban legends about things such as money-laundering schemes (how the mall supposedly got its start) to "gang fights" (how the mall supposedly met its demise).

Prior to its outright demise, this mall had always been attached to grand ideas rather than successful or reliable anchor stores. Romanian-born, Holocaust-surviving, Australian immigrant turned real estate mogul George Herscu dreamed up the original concept here. He had developed several other American malls of similar design, scope, and size, but when it came to Forest Fair Mall, critics decried the upscale stores as being unfit for the nearby blue-collar suburbs along the local beltway. Matters weren't helped by the fact that two large shopping malls existed just a few exits down the highway in each direction.

One of those nearby competitors was the Tri-County Mall. Just four miles east, this formerly outdoor shopping center underwent numerous renovations into the more typical indoor mall over the years. For decades it was bolstered by a revered local anchor and familiar global brands.

Even as Forest Fair went into yet another death spiral in the early aughts, Tri-County was known as one of the area malls still boasting the kinds of stores you and your friends liked. Teenagers could still clash with overzealous security guards and shop stores such as Aeropostale, Hollister, Abercrombie, and PacSun. The place even boasted the area's first Hot Topic, a store that once honored this author with a "District Employee of the Month" award.

But time has not been kind to Tri-County or most other area malls—though none has suffered a fate quite as brutal and decisive as Forest Fair.

The millennia-old concept of the arcade—a space lined with arches that combined the shelter of an indoor space with the airy expansiveness of an outdoor square—could be viewed as the historical precursor to what we know today as the twentieth-century shopping mall. The public market, the bazaar, a public place big enough for all, especially those with a little coin in their pocket for private commerce—that inspiration comes full circle at Forest Fair; even as indoor malls recede into the past tense, one of the few things remaining active here is an arcade, albeit a different kind than the place where you might have bought dates and fine tunic fabric in Roman times.

Video game parlors luring teenagers and their pocket change were a mainstay of any shopping palace, an essential attraction. Patrons of Pac-Man and Galaga probably weren't envisioned by Victor Gruen, the man widely regarded as the father of the American shopping mall, but then again, America's malls never really ended up aligning with his European-shopping-inspired concept anyways.

Forest Fair's current arcade, called Arcade Legacy, is a bit different from the traditional video game parlor. It's something of a simulacrum of the 1980s arcades popular during indoor malls' heydays. You pay a flat fee and then play to your heart's content, selecting from a plethora of now "vintage" games. Its location within a multi-story suburban shopping mall seems fitting but is likely born out of opportunity rather than nostalgia. Quite simply, this shopping center had plenty of space available, and this modern take on a retro arcade is one of the few things still bringing patrons in.

While the aforementioned arcade is well worth a visit on its own, the mall itself is the true draw. It's easy to poke fun at these decaying effigies to consumerism, but there's something more to this specific locale. The parking lines on the asphalt have long faded away, and the outside structure is dotted with peeling paint, graffiti, and the outlines of signs that remain after a business has left—the sight of dirt clinging to a cheap, fading facade, still stating "Babies 'R Us."

Finding which entrances are actually open is almost as challenging as any game in the arcade (the mall has no website, by the way, so rely on the arcade's for finding the building's hours). When you do make it inside, you'll be greeted by sweltering heat or shivering cold, as the building's HVAC system seems to have been cut off some time ago. The two remaining anchors and the handful of interior businesses seem to have their own climate control set up, but dress for the season, dear tourist.

You likely won't find yourself alone. Mall walkers getting their steps in are a common site, as are other curious sightseers, many of them locals reliving their personal memories of the place's former prominence.

Take heed as to not carry a "real" camera, and be subtle while using the one on your phone. The bicycle-riding security guards don't take kindly to anyone taking photographs, though they're just doing their jobs. Also be on the lookout for obstructions; many buckets (both the traditional yellow, mop variant and the orange "Home Depot" type) dot the landscape, catching water from the various leaks. Some of those are due to sections of skylights being completely smashed out by vandals.

Amazingly, despite this, a few businesses remain inside. There's a gym, a consignment shop, and a children's attraction erected on the site of the mall's former, second, short-lived indoor amusement park: a selection of inflatable "bounce castles" and slides to rent out for birthday parties.

The two remaining anchor stores, Kohl's and Bass Pro Shops, have their mall entrances sealed off. They exist on their own, physical connections severed.

It's not fair to compare this mall to either the original (1978) or remake (2004) *Dawn of the Dead* films. Those movies took place in active malls packed to the gills with things to buy. No, this place is overwhelmingly empty and has a much different apocalyptic vibe. Zombies didn't create this wasteland; poor market research followed by changing economic and consumer habits did.

Whether you grew up at this particular mall or came upon it as a visitor in its current state, there's a commonality to be found. Everyone will recognize the fading logos for Coca-Cola, Auntie-Anne's, and the Great Steak & Potato Company, even if the food court is empty and the vending machines are no longer stocked. If you need context, the mall's map will offer you a guide. Just be aware that it's now a piece of history highlighting what once *was* for a moment and is not actually informative.

A sculpted sign proudly stating "Ta-Da" still stands in one wing, a proclamation of the early 2000's Mills Corporation's renovation to show that yes, this mall had finally been saved. But even fifteen-year-old me knew that insect pet stores, such as "Bugz-N-Stuff," and the Big Dog T-shirt outlet were not positive signs of potential long-term business.

Forest Park/Fairfield: The Death and Life of American Malls

When I first became interested in the mall again as an adult, I was initially fooled by outward appearances. The stores lining the main road, standing independently in the parking lot, are popular and open. Chipotle, Starbucks, and Outback Steakhouse obscure the hulking structure behind them, itself relatively well maintained.

It wasn't until I moved back to the area and went for a jog around the building that I realized just how much was gone. Sears and Macy's left vacant anchor plots, and the parking garage was being used to store vehicles for nearby dealerships, giving a false impression of activity.

When I did make it inside, many hallmarks of a dying mall were present: power walkers, generic music blaring, and only a handful of businesses to be found—quite a few of them "dragon stores" (you know, the ones that sell those really large statues of dragons that you've never seen anyone buy).

A close friend of mine was recently struck with a similar urge to explore Tri-County Mall, the one just a few miles away. "Sterilized abandonment" is how he described the place. A few stores are attempting to hang on, but it's clear the mall is a far cry from its former self.

Still, the property's owners have at least made the decision to give the impression they're trying. The place is clean, well-lighted, and has an updated website, and if you went back in a time machine, it seems like it's just waiting on its tenants to arrive before a grand opening. For me, the feelings of walking through this particular mall are far more bittersweet than the previous. Unlike Forest Fair Village, this place isn't a ruin. It's very much intact, and if you squint your eyes, it feels like any other active mall. Hell, what was once the Disney Store still looks like a mid-nineties Disney Store.

Both of these past-their-prime shopping centers now serve as monuments to nostalgia. The trope of dead malls has been played out on the internet, in documentaries, and on Instagram, but they've transcended to something more in their current era.

These were places where people connected, eked out livings, got by, saw friends, said goodbyes, and experienced the full gamut of emotions. True, their unsustainable construction and proliferation isn't worth repeating (check back in twenty years for my piece on dying "lifestyle centers"), but these monuments in their current state are worth visiting while you still can. Whether you were old enough to know peak mall culture or not, the experience can only be fully realized in person rather than just through words or images. Go inside, think of the people, and maybe buy something if anyone's still selling.

Postscript: In 2022, local officials announced they had applied for state funds that could help facilitate the demolition of Forest Fair Mall/Cincinnati Mills. While the status of that application is unknown as of this writing (May 2022) and the mall presently remains accessible, the arcade has announced a relocation for the end of the summer. The spring of 2022 also brought confirmation of Tri-County's impending demise. The shopping center was slated to host its final day of business on May 15 as the local government prepared to move forward with a large-scale redevelopment plan for the site.

St. Bernard: Twenty-Four-Karat Service

NICOLE R. KLUNGLE

St. Bernard, Ohio, does not decorate its borders with conspicuous signs. During afternoon rush hour, if you have found yourself part of (or hindered by) the unrelenting stream of traffic turning left onto West Mitchell from Vine Street, you've passed St. Bernard's southwest corner, which features a low ornamental wall naming the village in understated brass letters. If you are driving west on Tennessee Avenue toward Vine, you might notice that the street name changes to Ross (and the speed limit goes down to twenty-five) at the intersection with Chalet.

That's really all the notice you'll get that you are passing out of Cincinnati and into an entirely separate municipality. Incorporated in 1878 by mostly German immigrants, the village was, for much of its early life, famed for Procter & Gamble's sprawling, castle-like Ivorydale soap facility, which was built in 1885 and employed 2,000 people—many St. Bernard residents—at its peak. (The Ivorydale facility continues to make soap for the St. Bernard Soap Company and boasts the largest rail yard in southwest Ohio for receiving raw materials.) St. Bernard's population swelled to more than 7,000 in the 1930s before falling in the second half of the twentieth century.

Today, the village boasts a population of about 4,300 people who enjoy their own police and fire departments, council and mayor, parks and recreation department, school district (shared with the adjacent village of Elmwood Place), and service department, which is equipped with a small fleet of trash and recycling trucks.

In fact, even if you've found yourself stuck behind one of St. Bernard's trash trucks, you've probably never thought much about them. Why would you? Trash gets picked up everywhere at least once a week. It's inevitable to find yourself stuck behind a trash truck at some point.

Except you are, in fact, twice as likely to get stuck behind a trash truck in St. Bernard. Our trash is picked up not once but twice per week.

Now, you may think I'm taking a swipe at the annoyance of getting stuck behind a slow-moving trash truck. Put that thought out of your mind.

What I am sharing with you is St. Bernard's twenty-four-karat secret, the true treasure of living in the 1.1-square-mile village of St. Bernard: the service department.

Yes, service department employees keep the flowers watered, the parks mowed, and the streets painted. Yes, they collect trash twice (and recycling once) a week. But if you will lend me your ear, I will convey to you the unmitigated luxury, the absolute poshness, of a service department that delivers dumpsters and dump trucks to residents for free use overnight or on the weekends. Give me a moment and I will take ten minutes to sing the praises of service department members who blatantly pamper residents by keeping their eyes peeled for furniture or appliances set out at the curb and sending trucks to collect them at no additional cost.

Layla Keiner, on the other hand, might also mention how difficult it is to get away with literally *anything* when everyone knows your dad, the garbageman.

Layla (née Helton) grew up in St. Bernard knowing—from experience—that any digression from family rules would be immediately conveyed to her dad, Bill, while he was out throwing garbage.

Her experiences highlight the second-most important thing you need to know about St. Bernard: The community has a closely held identity and a tight-knit culture. Layla, who grew up in St. Bernard and served as both class president and homecoming queen for the class of 2012 at St. Bernard–Elmwood Place High School, is conversant with both. People like me, who chose St. Bernard as their home at some point in their adult life, may find it difficult to break in. A significant percentage of St. Bernard's population consists of adults who, like Layla, were born in St. Bernard, grew up together, and have called it home for most of their lives. St. Bernard kids often stay or return as adults, even maintaining family homes—and family friendships—between generations. The adage "It's not what you know, it's who you know" is especially true here, where elected offices are de facto passed within multigenerational St. Bernard families.

When Layla goes for a walk, she can count on running into friends and neighbors to chat. A social media manager for Kroger, she has put her skills toward assisting with the political campaigns of both her mother, Sarah, and the current mayor, as well as marketing St. Bernard's Fresh Market, a pop-up market showcasing crafters, bakers, and other creators. (In fact, Layla is a founder and principal organizer of the Fresh Market.)

She's serving on the village's German Luau committee (St. Bernard hosts this annual celebration of lederhosen, Hawaiian shirts, and beer in August), and she's active with the village's Positive Action Committee, a group organized to host beneficial community events and activities. And she is unrelentingly positive about St. Bernard.

Her positivity is not unmerited. Layla appreciates St. Bernard's walkability, with a coffee shop, Wiedemann's Fine Beer, Skyline, Dairy Queen, and parks all easily accessible from anywhere in the village. I would be remiss not to mention that the public school system is in the process of building a new elementary and high school. St. Clement Elementary and Roger Bacon High School are also located here, to the benefit of the many Catholics in the area. The village is attracting new developments and eateries, and St. Bernard offers easy access to popular destinations in Northside, Clifton, Oakley, and Hyde Park, as well as to I-75 and the Norwood Lateral.

St. Bernard's many attractions aside, my experience has been that positivity is not only intrinsic to village identity and culture, it's *de rigueur*—especially among women. This can create an issue when legitimate critique is considered hostile or inappropriate; progress becomes impossible if everything is already perfect.

St. Bernard, as a whole, resists change. Its council recently rejected a nondiscrimination ordinance, for example, partially on the grounds that no such ordinance is needed in the already welcoming community. (Although people of the global majority make up about 20 percent of St. Bernard's population, the village council and administration are exclusively white, and a 2019 study by the Hamilton County Public Health Department found St. Bernard to be highly segregated.) Fortune-tellers and astrologists may not set up shop here. (You may be thinking that this prohibition must date back to more puritanical times. It was enacted in 2013.) It's telling that the one critique I hear consistently from lifetime St. Bernard residents is a wish for a return to a time when the village was even more close-knit.

Layla freely admits she is fortunate to circulate in a bubble of St. Bernard that quickly opens to new ideas and new people. Because her father is employed by the village and her mother ran for office, Layla has more insight into the village political scene than most. She acknowledges that small-town politics can be a popularity contest, with the same people running (and winning) over and over again. In fact, St. Bernard politics are remarkably isolated from the politics of the greater Cincinnati area; until recently, St. Bernard had its own political parties (technically, PACs that functioned as parties) that ran slates independently of the two traditional parties most of us are used to.

With that in mind, it's no surprise that the vision Layla holds for growth in the village includes a wish for more people to participate in crafting village policy and priorities. She also hopes St. Bernard will, as more and more families move into the area, become more open and inclusive of both new people and new ideas. I very much share these hopes.

In the meantime, I'm guessing that any shenanigans perpetrated by Layla's son, Louie, will be duly reported to Bill the garbageman.

Greenhills: Kneeling for Black Lives in a Town Born Segregated

NICK SWARTSELL

The grass was green on the commons in the heart of Greenhills, and its International Style Community Building shone white in the sunlight. It was a textbook early summer Friday in the quiet suburb just north of Cincinnati.

But June 5, 2020, was also unique.

Several dozen people, most but not all white, had just put down their Black Lives Matter signs and taken a knee in that grass around the gazebo that sits before the community building. For nine minutes—one for every minute white Minneapolis police officer Derek Chauvin held his knee to the neck of George Floyd on May 25 as Floyd, who was Black, died — there was nothing but the chirping of birds and the sound of traffic many yards away on Winton Road.

It was just nine minutes in the eighty-one-year existence of this small American village of about 3,600 people. But they were a poignant nine minutes, given the town's history.

As protests over the deaths of Floyd, Louisville's Breonna Taylor, and others rolled through many large American cities, drawing crowds of thousands, they also came—sometimes more slowly and quietly—to the nation's suburbs, including Greenhills.

The federal government created Greenhills in the depths of the Great Depression as one of President Franklin Delano Roosevelt's New Deal programs. It was one of three small towns designed to provide ideal, somewhat communal living for poor and working-class Americans who were suffering from the Depression and from the crowded, polluted conditions of cities like Cincinnati.

It was also expressly for whites only.

Long after the federal government divested from the town following World War II, that segregated legacy continued. Though a few Black students attended the village's school district prior, the district drew up a voluntary plan to integrate its high school in 1979, forty years after it was founded. But in 1984, the year after the first Black students brought in under that plan graduated, only twenty-three of Greenhills' 5,000 residents were Black.

Lisa Leace was one of those students. She grew up in neighboring Forest Park. For her, the rally on the green was a revelation. Wearing her Greenhills High School pride gear, Leace climbed into the gazebo and took a small bullhorn to praise both the organizers and attendees at the event—and pushed them to continue their work.

"Imagine my experience—Black people, whom Greenhills was not used to seeing, sent to a school with white students," she says. "We were not welcome. This would have never happened in 1983."

Greenhills has gotten more diverse in the years since Leace graduated—Black people account for about 13 percent of the village's population today. But a reputation for racial tension and disparities lingers among some in Greater Cincinnati, not helped by some unfortunate associations.

The last time Cincinnati saw massive protests over racial disparities in policing, they were sparked by the 2015 shooting of unarmed Black motorist Sam DuBose by former University of Cincinnati police officer Ray Tensing, who got his start as a part-time officer with the Village of Greenhills Police Department.

Greenhills residents, however, take pains to stress that it is a welcoming community. Black-owned businesses occupy the town's small business district. And like a lot of American suburbs, the village continues to diversify.

Some openly acknowledge its painful history with race, but they say they have hopes the town—and America as a whole—can transcend that history.

"This was a sundown town," says Pat Andwan, who has lived in Greenhills for decades and once ran for mayor. "That meant Blacks were not allowed in the town after sundown. I hope with the efforts of all the people here, their hearts and minds, things will change."

Danielle Horsley of neighboring Woodlawn spoke to the crowd at the rally before the moment of silence. She was one of four young, local organizers who put the rally together.

Horsley focused on the fact that June 5 was Taylor's birthday. Horsley said she identified with Taylor, who would be turning twenty-seven had she not died after Louisville police her shot eight times during a no-knock raid on her apartment. Taylor was not armed, though her boyfriend fired one round as police pounded down their door. Officers were serving a warrant on a person who did not live there and who turned out to already be in custody.

Horsley is twenty-six, like Taylor was at the time of her death. Like Taylor, Horsley is Black.

Three other organizers—Tahji Woods of neighboring Forest Park, and Greenhills' Nick Purdin and Susie Lutes—asked Horsley to come speak.

"I didn't expect anyone to join us, but it turned into a great thing," Purdin said. "I value these people because they've spoken some great words."

Woods has both positive and negative associations with Greenhills, including some experiences with racism, he says.

"This was my roaming ground growing up," he says. "I stayed in Forest Park, but I was always over here meeting people at the pool. We used to meet up here and play football. I really did feel the need to mention the injustices that have happened in this community."

Susie Lutes is the fourth member of the group that organized the event. Like Purdin, she grew up in Greenhills.

"I couldn't ignore it," she said of the protests happening across the country over racial disparities. "We had to bring it here to our town. We wanted to bring it to the smaller communities, where it is easier to look away and not pay attention. People are just going to the pool and living like normal. We wanted to put it in peoples' faces who aren't paying attention."

But the message that day on the sunny green was one of understanding, too. It is understandable to be overwhelmed about America's racial tensions, organizers told the crowd. Everyone is still learning.

"It's OK not to know," Horsley told the crowd. "I understand that when tensions rise, it's hard to listen. You feel attacked. You're going to feel attacked—trust me, I know. But it's about stepping out of that, removing yourself from that emotion. We have to be willing to learn from each other and teach each other. It's OK to say, 'I have no idea what is going on, but I know this is not right.' I will not judge you. I will support you, as long as there is genuine support for me."

Those who came out to the event were largely receptive.

Greenhills-Winton Woods School District educator Gary Giblin has taught middle school just down the street from the rally location for two decades.

"We're privileged to be here," he told organizers. "Thank you for stepping up here and speaking. You made me want to cry. I'm an old white guy . . . and I'm embarrassed. But I want to tell you that we're learning. At a time when Black lives don't seem to matter, we need to say, 'Black lives matter.'"

Norwood:
A Kingdom Unto Itself
ANGELA PANCELLA

Tucked away at the end of a residential street in West Norwood is a small neighborhood park called Upper Millcrest. (There is also a Lower Millcrest, joined to its neighbor by wooden stairs and an unnamed mezzanine populated by dinosaur playground equipment, but these do not enter the story.) Buried not far beneath the soil, locals claim, is rubble from the houses that were torn down to make way for the stores of Rookwood Commons and Pavilion—the outdoor shopping destinations many Cincinnatians flock to for organic juice from Whole Foods or khakis from the Gap.

In the northernmost portion of Norwood, just south of the Cincinnati neighborhood of Pleasant Ridge, a long fortress of a building with a commanding view stands with a mansion just behind it. The more imposing structure was a Catholic seminary; the mansion was built to be the residence of the archbishop of Cincinnati. The archbishop of the time expected Norwood, as a small independent city, to be annexed by the larger metropolis. That never happened, so the story goes that the archbishop never moved in.

Norwood still isn't part of Cincinnati municipally, though it is the second-largest city in Hamilton County. It is to Cincinnati as Vatican City is to Rome—surrounded by the larger city, but a kingdom unto itself. People living there refer to it as "the center of the universe"; remarkably, for a 3.1-square-mile city with a little fewer than 20,000 inhabitants, it seems everyone knows someone with a Norwood connection.

To live in this city-within-a-city is to experience being known, once you start getting engaged in the place. Robert Putnam would delight in this town: Norwood is the place the "Bowling Alone" phenomenon forgot. Longstanding civic organizations, like the Norwood Business and Professional Women's Club, the Eagles, and the Moose Lodge keep on keeping on, while newer groups like Norwood Together organize park cleanups and walks on the Wasson Way bike trail, and prepare welcome bags to give to new neighbors.

On the fourth Tuesday of every July (barring pandemics), the whole city lines Montgomery Road to cheer for the Norwood Day Parade, a cavalcade of fire trucks, Shriners, marching bands, and floats, the last of which, of course, includes the cow mascot of United Dairy Farmers, headquartered in town. UDF's founder, one Carl Lindner, was the patriarch of one of Cincinnati's foremost business dynasties, which is now worth billions.

An Indigenous earthwork overlooking the heart of the city (and the surging Norwood lateral, which carries traffic between Cincinnati's major highways, I-71 and I-75) is a mute testament to the region's first peoples. More recent settlement by whites began sometime in the early 1800s. By 1809, what is now Norwood was a few houses huddled together under the name Sharpsburg. Sixty years and a railroad depot later, Norwood had its current name.

Since that time, the city has had a stubborn, independent streak. In the early twentieth century, Norwood residents twice resisted annexation by the city of Cincinnati, though by the slimmest of margins. A century later, three homeowners who were huddled on land across from the aforementioned shopping mega-center, Rookwood Commons, fought Norwood all the way to the Ohio Supreme Court to keep their houses out of the clutches of eminent domain as a developer tried to build another shopping center on the land. The state's high court ruled in their favor, and it wasn't until the last capitulated three years later—and sold his house for a cool $1.25 million—that work on the next shopping center began.

Norwood's past is always just under the surface or hiding in plain sight. But where there is rubble or abandoned plans, there is also transformation. The seminary and would-be archbishop's residence is now a retreat center. Upper Millcrest is now full of produce plots: tomatoes, peppers, and butternut squash, grown for community-supported agriculture (a CSA).

In days gone by, Norwood was the butt of jokes that may have arisen through stereotypes associated with factory towns, or with towns with shuttered factories (its economic base for many years was a sprawling General Motors plant, which rolled out its last Camaro in 1987). This easy dismissal by the outside world, and this occasional stubbornness, created a space in which Norwood could just be itself—largely working-class and blue-collar, but with the occasional hidden mansion.

Lockland: Rust Belt Dream Come True

ALEXANDER C. SMITH

You could say that the small industrial city just north of Cincinnati called Lockland was historically lucky in one sense. It had two great heydays of great prosperity and prominence, when not every place even gets one. They both ended, decades ago, and even the physical remnants of both are now gone.

But there is a new energy growing, bit by bit, brought here by folks from across the world.

In the late nineteenth and early twentieth centuries, the Miami and Erie Canal ran through here, with the locks for which Lockland is named serving to let cargo boats pass through on their way to the Ohio River. Now? The canal path is I-75, which you can traverse on your way to someplace else.

Later, after the canal was no longer relevant, Lockland had a great industrial boom following World War II. Outfits like Jefferson Smurfit, Celotex, the Philip Carey Company, American Tissue, and the greatest of all, the Stearns & Foster mattress firm, provided well-paying employment for generations of families.

Every one of them has been out of business for many years, and all their buildings have been knocked down, leaving only empty lots. Stearns & Foster, in particular, left behind enormous brownfields on either side of Shepherd Avenue, which are now primarily grounds for illegal dumping. In fact, on a recent walk, I saw a mattress there, forlorn in the weeds, but it was a Sealy.

No, this doesn't seem like the ideal historical moment to visit Lockland. But it is still a place where people live, and it's still a place that some people love. And if you look closely, you can see new signs of life springing up.

I went to Wolfman's Tavern—the absolute last survivor of the era when there was a bar on every street to serve thirsty workmen after their shifts—hoping to talk to somebody who remembered a bit of the good old days.

But Barb the bartender told me all the old-timers have passed on. The closest she and patrons could give me of a sense of the grandeur of those times was the way they described how Stearns & Foster's 1.2-million-square-foot plant loomed over the neighborhood.

"It rose up over everything—blocked out the sun in here," she said.

But Barb's favorite Stearns story was of when half the place burned down in 2004. It took out the power for blocks around. The denizens of Wolfman's drank in the dark.

I asked if there was any buzz locally about businesses interested in buying the lot, but she told me frankly, "There hasn't been anything for a while, and I don't think there's going to be."

On first glance, that's the sense you get about all of Lockland's central business district. To be sure, on the blocks nearby, there are plenty of lovingly maintained old houses where the daffodils are springing up even now. But the central square gives off an overpowering sense of a town that's lost its reason for being. Welling's, Shelly's, Vaughn-Hesley, Merkle's Meats: you can see these signs still, on buildings that the businesses moved out of before the turn of this century. The 1942 WPA Guide to Cincinnati described Lockland as "a noisy place filled with bustling traffic"; when I went out walking on a pleasant Sunday afternoon, I did not see a single soul. And after all—where would they be going?

Still, it's not all doom and gloom. If your idea of heaven is a street lined with trendy boutiques, artisanal cafes, and gastropubs—well, you'll be waiting a long time for that to come to Lockland. (Of course, you can just cross the railroad tracks into Wyoming if that's what you want—they've already got it there.) But if you head west out of the central business district on Wayne Avenue, you start to see unmistakable signs of life.

Over by the post office, you've got the Church of Christ, Lockland, and Lockland Church of the Nazarene still pulling in congregations, and the beautifully preserved Roettger Stadium, home of the Lockland High Panthers. Keep going and you encounter a veterinarian's office, a couple of auto mechanics' shops, the sharply painted Clean Cut barber shop, a shiny new True Value hardware store. Still there are the empty storefronts and potholed roads, but there are also people doing business, money changing hands.

And as you cross over Wayne Avenue, you'll start to see fresher energy. Signs in red, green, and yellow: Teddungal Fuuta International Market, Pam Adama Convenience Store, African-Arabian Fashion & Cosmetics, Touba Teddungal Restaurant. Even experienced travelers might not recognize these names—I certainly had to ask, and I found that these few blocks are the foothold of Cincinnati's Senegalese community.

Walk into Touba Teddungal and let Ace spoon you up a tray of *thiebu djeun* with a cup of hot *cafe Touba*, and take your seat; and as you eat, you'll witness ten or twelve or fifteen people from West African countries pass through, stopping to chat for a minute before they head back out to work. It really was a "noisy place filled with bustling traffic," come to Lockland again.

Ace was happy to see a new face, and happy to tell me all about Senegalese cuisine; he implored me to keep coming back until I had tried all twenty-four of their special dishes, pictured in colorful printouts that covered a whole wall.

"I like Lockland," he told me. "You see all these empty businesses? Offices? Houses? We can buy these cheap, much cheaper than in other places. One day these can be all Senegal businesses." Why not? Right now, it's just these two blocks north and south of Wayne Avenue, but goodness knows there's plenty of room to expand into. One man's Rust Belt bad dream could someday be another's dream come true.

Contributors

Jon Carter is a visual artist who currently lives and paints in Cincinnati. His artistic practice involves explorations of the urban environment in oil and mixed media. He grew up in the inner city and also lived there as an adult for quite some time. The markets, outdoor dining spots, pubs, and smells of these areas fire his imagination.

Rev. Alan Dicken lives in Mount Auburn with his family. He serves as the associate director for immigrant and refugee response for the Christian Church (Disciples of Christ). He loves Cincinnati, and it will always be his home.

Eric Eble teaches at a local all-boys Catholic school and resides in Madisonville with eight chickens, two dogs, and two cats, who all entertain his two children and keep his one partner and him very busy. He also writes poetry and coaches high school speech and debate.

Katrina Eresman is a freelance writer and musician based in Cincinnati, Ohio. She is the author of an ongoing series of microessays called *Disco Diaries*. You can find that, and more of her work, at katrinaeresman.com.

Gail Finke is a writer, radio producer, and aspiring novelist who lives in a College Hill development that was a plant nursery until the 1930s. Her book, *Images of America: College Hill*, is available from Arcadia Publishing.

Jocelyn Gibson is a Camp Washington Resident and city planner. She is on the neighborhood's community council and is active in the neighborhood's community garden. Jocelyn is originally from Ontario, Canada, and originally moved to Ohio to attend the University of Cincinnati. For her employment, she consults on municipal land use and zoning policy and how they can more effectively center equity and resiliency.

Liz Gottmer is a writer and housing advocate at Cincinnati's Peaslee Center. She hails from four generations of Mount Adams residents but currently lives on a different high point—East Price Hill—with her housemates and her dog, Lou.

Greg Hand is proprietor of the *Cincinnati Curiosities* blog, retired from the University of Cincinnati as associate vice president for public relations. Before his employment by the university, Hand was editor of the Western Hills Press in suburban Cincinnati. Among his activities in the Westwood neighborhood, Hand serves as president of the Westwood Community Urban Redevelopment Corporation (WestCURC).

Pauletta Hansel served as Cincinnati's first poet laureate and is 2022 writer in residence for the Public Library of Cincinnati and Hamilton County. Her newest poetry collection is *Heartbreak Tree*, an exploration of the intersection of gender and place in Appalachia. Her writing has been featured in *Oxford American*, *Rattle*, *American Life in Poetry*, and *Poetry Daily*, among others.

Michael Henson is the author of five books of fiction and four collections of poetry. *Maggie Boylan*, a collection of linked stories, won recognition for its depiction of a woman's struggles with poverty and addiction in rural Appalachia. His latest is *Secure the Shadow*, a novel.

Bonnie Speeg Holliday is from Cincinnati, but she has lived across the United States since 1953. She traces the past into the present through words. Her work is found at tracingpaperblog.wordpress.com. Her favorite works are her artistic children.

Deqah Hussein-Wetzel is a podcaster and historic preservationist based in Cincinnati, Ohio. She is the cofounder of Urbanist Media and the cohost and coproducer of the Urban Roots podcast.

Nicole R. Klungle is a freelance book editor and a local advocate for government transparency and best practices. She has lived in St. Bernard for a mere twenty-one years.

Dani McClain reports on race and parenting and served as the Cincinnati Public Library's writer in residence in 2020 and 2021. McClain's book, *We Live for the We: The Political Power of Black Motherhood*, was published in 2019 by Bold Type Books and was shortlisted in 2020 for a Hurston/Wright Legacy Award.

Angela Pancella lived fourteen years in Norwood, Ohio, and now refers to Cincinnati as "Greater Norwood." She is a past director of Woven Oak Initiatives, a nonprofit dedicated to offering small community-serving programs a place to thrive, and she helped launch Norwood Together, a CDC whose mission is to grow and build equitable economic and community development in the city. Now living in St. Louis, Missouri, she continues to make regular pilgrimages back to the center of the universe.

Rob Pasquinucci is a public relations professional and is the current president of the Mount Lookout Community Council. He lives in Mount Lookout with his wife, Sarah and sons Robert and Samuel.

Cailin Pitt is an artist and software engineer in Atlanta, Georgia. He is a former resident of Cincinnati, Ohio.

Carrie Rhodus is a historian and historic preservationist who has worked as a teacher, draftsperson, realtor, and community surveyor. She currently serves as the operations manager for the Jewish Cemeteries of Greater Cincinnati. She is also a cofounder and board president of Urbanist Media, an antiracist community preservation consulting and empowerment nonprofit based in Cincinnati.

Briana Rice is a reporter who grew up in Greater Cincinnati. She graduated from the School for Creative and Performing Arts and the University of Cincinnati. Her favorite places in the area are Findlay Market, the Mercantile Library, and any place serving Cincinnati-style veggie chili.

Ronny Salerno is a photographer and author of two books: *The Future is One of Mighty Ducks T-Shirts and Discmen* (2013) and *Fading Ads of Cincinnati* (2015). Currently working on two new publications, he regularly publishes stories at RonnySalerno.com.

Caitlyn Short grew up just outside of Cincinnati's neighborhoods but continues to explore all fifty-two of them since the day she learned to drive. She often spends her free time photographing the city's skyline from its many hilly vistas. At home, you can find her in her garden, hot cup of coffee in hand while oldies or soul music plays on the radio.

Anne Skove was born and raised in Clifton. Even though the house is close enough to the zoo (Avondale) that a runaway monkey once called her attic home, it's in Clifton. Although she moved away for a few decades, now three generations of her family live in the same house she (and the monkey) grew up in.

Alexander C. Smith was born in Nashville, Tennessee, and settled in Ohio in 2018. He hopes to be the last man to leave Forest Fair Village on the day when they close it for good, and he still remembers where he was when the Hartwell Gold Star burned down. He lives in Springfield Township, near, but not in, one of Galbraith Road's legendary potholes.

Anne Delano Steinert is a visiting assistant professor of history at the University of Cincinnati, where she also directs the Center for the City. She studies the built environment with a focus on late nineteenth- and early twentieth-century Cincinnati. Steinert is the founding board chair of the Over-the-Rhine Museum and was the curator of the *Look Here!* (2015), *Schools for the City* (2016), and *Finding Kenyon Barr* (2017) exhibitions. Steinert was cocreator of the New Deal Neighbors oral history project in Greenhills, Ohio, and is currently coordinating the Avondale Neighborhood History Initiative. Her most challenging job is being mom to her son Seneca, who loves the stone slide in Burnet Woods.

Nick Swartsell is a journalist and photographer based in Cincinnati. He lived in Mount Auburn for eight years before moving to Camp Washington while editing this book.

Sarah Thomas is the proud granddaughter of Lebanese immigrants. She lives in Cincinnati, Ohio, with her partner and daughter. Her work in housing and community development is driven by the belief that we all deserve to live a dignified life. Sarah maintains a lifelong affinity for cooking and sharing meals, finds pure joy in her rescue dog, Vada, and enjoys the freedom of traveling.

Katie Vogel is the deputy editor of SEO at *USA Today*. She lives in Northside with her husband, her flock of chickens, and several hives of bees.

Thurman Wenzl is a retired public health scientist in worker protection, and a volunteer organizer for worker centers in the Cincinnati area and Chicago.

Annette J. Wick is a writer, teacher, public speaker, and author of *I'll Have Some of Yours*, a memoir of cookies and caregiving. She's a combination of Italian roots, small-town footholds, and urban living, with writings that span the arts, cities, women's issues, aging, and memory. Visit annettejwick.com to read more.

Kathy Y. Wilson is a multihyphenated nerd: a writer-teacher-closet-poet-community-worker-playwright and sometimes, for the right audience, she will bust a rhyme. She was twice a fellow at the Knight Center for Professional Journalists and was a finalist for a National Magazine Award. She sometimes works on her next book, *The Dialysis Diaries: How Hattie McDaniel Taught Me to Pee Again*. In September 2014, the Library Foundation of the Public Library of Cincinnati and Hamilton County named her its first-ever writer in residence. She lives in downtown East Walnut Hills with her partner and a cornucopia of Black Barbie dolls.

Dann Woellert is an avid preservationist and historian. He writes the blog *Dann Woellert the Food Etymologist* and has authored seven books on regional food history.

Elissa Yancey is a Norwood native and Urban Appalachian writer, educator, and nonprofit leader. Through a career as a journalist, teacher, author, and mom, she has embraced plenty of obstacles on her journey to connect people through story and action.

Julie Zimmerman is a longtime resident of North Avondale who has written for local and national publications. A California native, she moved to Cincinnati in 1995, intending to stay two to three years.

www.ingramcontent.com/pod-product-compliance
Lightning Source LLC
Chambersburg PA
CBHW030900170426
43193CB00009BA/681